CW01500230

MAP

THE POETRY OF
Chiyo-ni

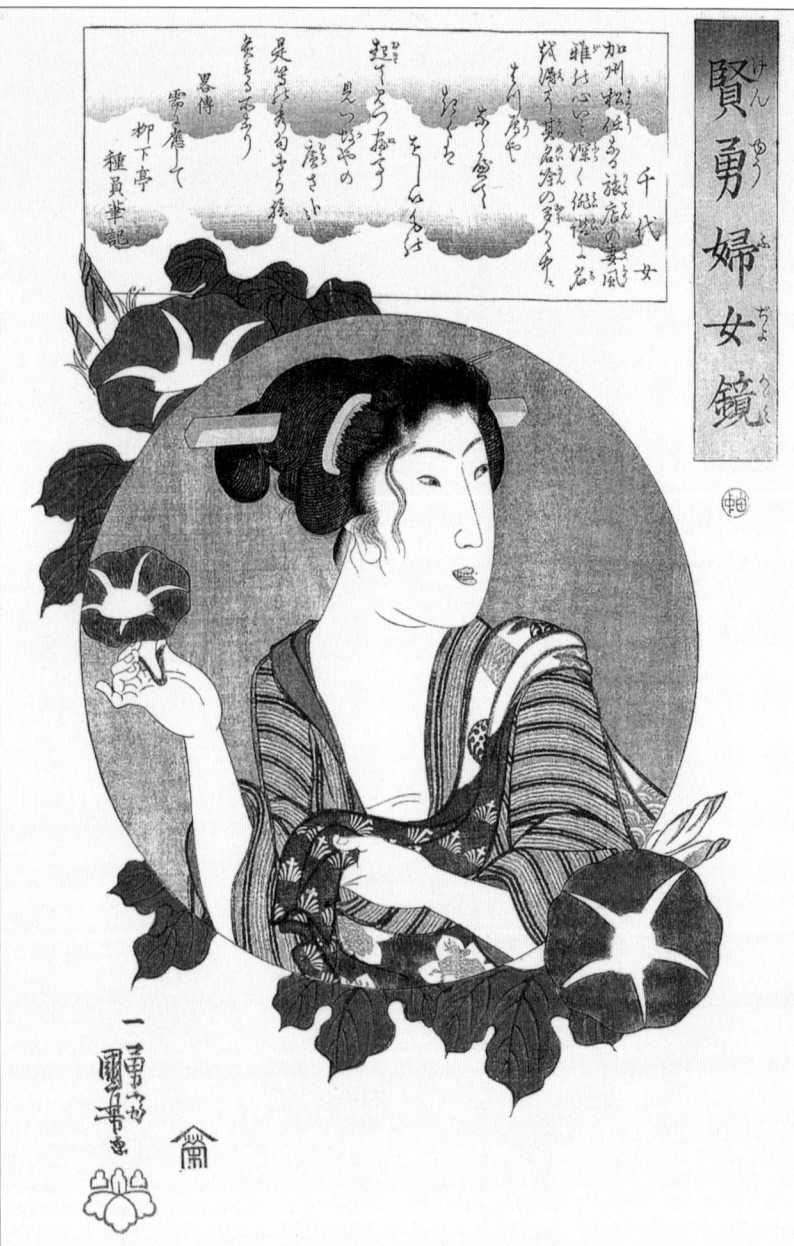

THE POETRY OF
Chiyo-ni

The Life and Art *of* Japan's Most Celebrated Woman Haiku Master

PATRICIA DONEGAN

YOSHIE ISHIBASHI

FOREWORD BY NATALIE GOLDBERG

TUTTLE Publishing

Tokyo │ Rutland, Vermont │ Singapore

To all women haijin (haiku poets)
known and unknown
who lived the way of haiku
or
who are now living the way of haiku

Contents

LIST OF ILLUSTRATIONS

ACKNOWLEDGMENTS

Foremost acknowledgment to the Fulbright Foundation for their support of Patricia Donegan's grant project to complete this book.

The Museum and Library of Haiku Literature (Haiku Bungakukan) in Tokyo was the center for our translations and research. We wish to express our gratitude to Dr. Kazuo Sato, haiku poet and director of the International Division, for his constant generosity as Patricia's Fulbright advisor, and for serving as our haiku teacher and translation consultant. Thanks to the staff there as well.

Our grateful acknowledgment to haiku poet and haiku ambassador Kristen Deming for her careful editing of the manuscript.

Special thanks to *renku* poet Tadashi Kondo, president of the Association of International Renku, for initially interpreting the *renku* and guiding us in writing *renku*. Thanks also to poet-artist Kris Kondo for checking the haiku translations, along with Eiko Yachimoto.

We would also like to recognize the haiku poet Suzuko Shinagawa, a disciple of the late haiku master Seishi Yamaguchi, for deepening our understanding of Chiyo-ni's *renku* and our writing of *renku* as well.

Thanks to Barbara Plante, Rights and Reproductions Director of the Museum of Fine Arts in Springfield, Massachusetts for borrowed artwork. Thanks also to Patricia Fister for sharing her Chiyo-ni research materials. To Norma Burton for suggestions on the manuscript. To Yoshiko Amemiya and Liya Yang for background information. To Anthony Walter of Caliburn, who saved our computer's life several times. And thanks to our editors at Charles E. Tuttle Company for guiding this book to completion.

We also wish to express our gratitude to the following people in Matto, Japan, for showing us Chiyo-ni's original artwork and allowing us to reprint these illustrations: Nobutaka Aoki, Genji Kimura, Kenji Miyaho, Mrs. Shiromaru, and Mitsuo Tanaka; as well as the following public sponsors: Osamu Nakano, chief of Shokoji temple; Hideo Nakatani, Masae Nagai, and Hiroaki Kaneyama, curators of the Matto City Museum. Thanks also to Kimiaki Tokuda, librarian of the Central Matto Library, and to Kikumaro Tokuda, who supplied us with research materials on Chiyo-ni and opened many doors for us; Tatsuo Wakamizu of Matto City Hall; and finally to Kiyoko Nakamoto, for permission to reprint from her late husband's books.

Finally, Yoshie wishes to express appreciation to her family and friends for their encouragement, and to Satoshi Osawa for his support of this project. Patricia expresses her deepest gratitude to her parents, Janet and Dan Donegan, for their belief in her path and for insights on this book when it was a work-in-progress; and to family and friends.

FOREWORD

A number of years ago, this book went out of print and became a precious item. I am so glad that Tuttle Publishing has had the good sense to reissue this Japanese woman's haiku. She is considered equal to the great Master Basho, the originator of this form. He strapped a satchel on his back and walked with a friend for six months, recording a journal with intermittent haiku, entitled *Narrow Road to the Deep North*.

No ordinary Japanese woman was allowed this freedom, though Chiyo-ni was considered as talented a haiku writer. She found her own way, and at fifty-two, when her familial responsibilities were complete, she became a nun. She did not join a monastery, but a Buddhist nun in Japan was free to travel on her own. Like Basho, she had a coterie of students—women who cared about poetry, writing and haiku, that three-line form that drops the reader and writer into an immense world, using the ordinary present specific life in front of you, nothing special but illuminating the depth of a human and non-human life.

Just last week a student leaving for a three-month retreat at Tassajara Zen monastery dropped off this precious book I had lent him—he was afraid it would be lost or damaged. Now he, a potter and baker, was joining his twin, a young woman, to practice with intensity together in California. He had originally offered me a haiku booklet to read, written by him and his sister.

"I don't want to lose the book. I know it's rare," Henry told me.

"You can borrow it again when you come back."

I had been lucky enough to know Patricia Donegan briefly at

Naropa Institute in Boulder, so when she and Yoshie Ishibashi traveled down to New Mexico in 1999 for a book signing I purchased the book and had them sign it.

Standing in the doorway at the Taos reading, I opened to the dedication: *To all women haijin (haiku poets) / known and unknown / who lived the way of haiku / or / who are now living the way of haiku…*

Considering this dedication, how could it ever have gone out of print? Japanese women took courage and wrote their own unique haiku. We didn't in the West know this. Tuttle Publishing has seized the moment, and *hallelujah*, is republishing it, so when Henry is buffered by all that meditation deep in the Carmel Valley and when the three months are finished and he returns to the Upaya Zen Center down the road, I can hand him and his twin their own copies.

Until that time, I can read Chiyo-ni, but where are the other Japanese women in haiku? The key is translation. Patricia, who died a short while ago, needed Yoshie and together they gave the Western world—and women—Chiyo-ni. I have many volumes of Basho, but translation is a difficult thing. How beautiful to have the two women work on translation together. It's not as simple as eight apples weigh the same in another language and country. The two women had to transmit the flavor, spirit, vitality, nuance of Chiyo-ni's haiku to her new Western audience. Women need to experience her passion, her live intuition and leap into the faith that her way of seeing can be communicated.

I listened in poetry class in 1976 when Allen Ginsberg, who I loved, espoused great male poets and I was certain there must be great women poets. Women were at least half the population. Certainly Chiyo-ni knew this too, took courage along the way and saw haiku's possibility. Even more important, Chiyo-ni lived the Way of Haiku, a way of life, as a path of awakening. In ancient Japan to become a nun, she was allowed to choose not to live in a nunnery, but to travel freely among poets, and nature, to walk with the moon in sight, along rivers, streams and ponds.

During Covid, haiku brought solace to many readers. When I led a group of writing students to Japan, we all wanted to visit Matto, where she lived and where Shoko-ji Temple was dedicated to her. I was sick on the day we visited and could not go, but the writers eagerly told me of the haiku written in her own hand.

I had the pleasure to go again with a group of calligraphers in 2023 with Kaz Tanahashi. Again we scheduled a visit to her temple, wedged between an overnight stay at Eiheiji, Dogen's solemn and beautiful monastery established in 1244 and D.T. Suzuki's austere, graceful museum. In comparison, Shoko-ji Temple, dedicated to a woman poet, was more relaxed. We noted a square flower arrangement, something we'd never seen in the West; a dragon, belching water into a pool and two buxom women in a framed scroll. It was fun to wander around a place where creativity could happen, where we weren't so intimidated by making a mistake in formalities.

Etchings were on the big bell, based on original pictures by the famous woodblock artist Munakata Shiko, something unusual marking the reverence Chiyo-ni had as a haiku poet.

Please enjoy this book. Realize that reading haiku is a refuge when your mind and your world feel out of kilter. Read the haiku aloud, each one, more than once. They are Chiyo-ni's own, written a long time ago, but most important, they speak to us now:

> a hundred gourds
> from the heart
> of one vine

Can you be that vine?
Yes, a woman is allowed to believe in herself.

Natalie Goldberg
Author of *Three Simple Lines* and *Writing on Empty*

PREFACE

It is deep in a midsummer night, in a small village in eighteenth-century Japan. A candle burns low. Chiyo-ni, a young woman poet, sits on a temple mat, looking intently into the darkness. She is meditating on the theme, *hototogisu* (the cuckoo or nightingale), given to her by her haiku master. She has already attempted several poems, but all were rejected by her master as contrived. Perhaps there is a moon. Perhaps there isn't. Everything is still.

The paper screen begins to light up faintly. Finally the dawn comes and a bird cries out. At that moment Chiyo-ni awakens—she is not conscious of herself, but only of the bird and the dawn. She is completely open to the moment, and finally writes what's known as her first "enlightenment" haiku, a haiku without artifice or comment—just the perception and bare recording of that moment: "repeating / *hototogisu, hototogisu–* / day dawned." More than two hundred years pass. It is the early 1970s, and I am reading a description of that moment in D. T. Suzuki's book *Zen and Japanese Culture*. I am moved by Chiyo-ni's voice and story of awakening, which remained as fresh as that moment. And although I later found that this particular story was a myth, it was my doorway to her world.

I was moved to find a record of a woman haiku poet's spiritual journey, which continued to haunt me for years. I was excited because I had found what seemed to be the female counterpart to Basho, Japan's most famous male haiku poet. And although every Japanese poetry anthology in English that I picked up mentioned that Chiyo-ni (1703–75) was Japan's most famous woman haiku poet, and included a few of her haiku, there was virtually no information on her in English—unlike her male counterparts Basho, Buson, and Issa.

Later, while teaching courses on comparative poetry from the East and West at Naropa Institute from 1976 to 1985, I was shocked by the lack of translations of works by Japanese female poets. There were only a few books, like Kenneth Rexroth and Ikuko Atsumi's collection *The Burning Heart: Women Poets of Japan*, exclusively devoted to women poets; or hard-to-find translations of *Tangled Hair*, by Akiko Yosano, a twentieth-century tanka poet. At that time I vowed to do a translation of Chiyo-ni and other women haiku poets, to fill part of the void. Twenty years later, there are more books in translation, but there is a need for more. In fact, my co-translator and I are preparing an anthology of women poets of the Basho school.

But it wasn't until I returned to Japan in 1986–87, to study with haiku master Seishi Yamaguchi and to research Chiyo-ni's haiku, that I discovered what an important writer she is. Not only had she written 1,700 haiku (on average, haiku poets write about one thousand in a lifetime) but had published two collections of her haiku—an unusual feat for a woman of eighteenth-century Japan. But unlike most of the women poets, there was a wealth of stories about Chiyo-ni's life, which made her almost as well known as Basho. She was a celebrity in her time. There were other women *haijin* (haiku poets) as great as Chiyo-ni and perhaps even greater—and because this point could be argued at great length, let us simply say that Chiyo-ni exemplifies the best women *haijin* of the Edo period (1603–1867). But more importantly, I discovered that the reason Chiyo-ni was so known and respected was because she had lived the Way of Haiku. Haiku was an "awareness practice" for her, an integral part of her everyday life.

It was at this point that I fortunately met Yoshie Ishibashi, an innately gifted translator and researcher. Initially she was my translator for Seishi Yamaguchi's haiku classes, yet soon wanted to share Chiyo-ni's vision as much as I did—and so our collaboration began. Interestingly, when we began translating Chiyo-ni's haiku I began dreaming about the poet, and her words from those dreams inspired and guided our book:

> Appreciate each moment; that's all there really is. Be simple. Let my haiku teach you how. Openness is all you need to understand my haiku. Be open to each ringing of the bell, each kiss, each pain, each word, each wind. Follow the fearless path of white light, which covers everything, washes everything clean and white and illuminated like clear water—drink the sweet water!

However, for seven years the Chiyo-ni book was on the back burner, until I received a Fulbright grant in 1994–95. In the spring of that year, on the day our book was accepted for publication, we had an interesting experience. On the way to our publishers' office in Tokyo, Yoshie and I met an old Buddhist nun in white robes, dressed like Chiyo-ni might have dressed two hundred years ago. She was lost and we helped her find her way; her presence also helped us—it felt like an auspicious heralding of the book, and reassured us. Later in the year, when visiting Shokoji temple, which Chiyo-ni had frequented long ago, we felt her strong presence. I wrote the following haiku to commemorate the occasion: "incense / at Shokoji temple / Chiyo-ni's still breathing." We can only hope that something of her vision still breathes through our translations.

ON OUR TRANSLATIONS

This is the first book of English translations devoted to a woman haiku master. And this is the first time that Chiyo-ni's entire biography, literary criticism of her work, examples of her *renku* (linked-verse series), *haibun*, and approximately two hundred of her haiku have been translated into English. Nearly three-fourths of the haiku have never been translated before. Only about fifty of her haiku, out of a canon of 1,700, have been previously translated into English by others over the years. The first translation of a Chiyo-ni haiku—her famous morning glory haiku—appeared in B. H. Chamberlain's *A Handbook of Colloquial Japanese* (1898). Chamberlain used this poem, when introducing haiku to Westerners, as a prime example of the genre in his famous essay, "Basho and the Japanese Poetical Epigram," which he presented at an Asiatic Society of Japan meeting in 1902. Remarkably, it has taken one hundred years since her poetry was first translated for a volume of her haiku to be published in English.

Most translations of her work during this one-hundred-year interim are scattered in various anthologies (see starred items in bibliography), primarily Miyamori's *An Anthology of Haiku Ancient and Modern* (1932), R. H. Blyth's *History of Haiku* (vol. 1, 1963), Hiroaki Sato and Burton Watson's *From the Country of Eight Islands* (1981), and Patricia Fister's *Japanese Women Artists* (1989). One comment about R. H. Blyth. Even though I feel indebted to him and he remains one of the most respected translators of haiku, his derogatory comments about female haiku poets in *History of Haiku*—"it is doubtful whether women can write haiku" and "haiku poetesses are only fifth class"—surely contributed to their neglect and limited translation over the years.

Yet, we discovered that before Blyth there was interest in Chiyo-ni among a few European women translators. One find was a French doctoral thesis on Chiyo-ni, *Une poetesse japonaise au IVIII siecle, Kaga no Tchiyo-jo* by Gilberte Hla-Dorge, published in Paris in 1936. It includes background on Chiyo-ni, plus translations of many of her haiku. Why this thesis never became a book or why it was never translated into English remains a mystery; we also found that in the 1980s, when Hla-Dorge was in her late eighties, she visited Japan and Chiyo-ni's grave at the temple museum in Matto. During one of our visits there in 1994, the head abbot told us about Hla-Dorge so, indirectly, our paths crossed. Another find was an anthology, *Master Singers of Japan*, published in London in 1910 and edited by an Englishwoman, Clara Walsh. It contains several of her translations of Chiyo-ni's haiku. Our book is really a continuation of this interest in Chiyo-ni's life and haiku. Hopefully, others will translate more of her work, as well as that of other women haiku masters. And, hopefully, it won't take another hundred years.

Translation is said to be like a kiss through a veil. Even while we acknowledge that there is no perfect translation, we feel humbled, as most translators do, by the limitations of capturing the nuance of the original language. Japanese is especially difficult, as it relies so much upon the power of suggestion and the subtlety of emotion. Hopefully, there is something in poetry which, though expressed in words, ultimately goes beyond words—some essence of transcendental mystery or truth that each poet, in his or her best moments, taps into. It is this essence which, we hope, though distilled in a different form, still remains.

We have tried to keep our translations as faithful to the original as possible, taking out nothing, adding nothing; however, what may make perfect sense in Japanese often needs too much explanation in English and loses the poignancy and magic of the original. Because we want to be clear, but not destroy the elusive, we relied upon notes only when clarification was necessary; yet, it was our intention to make each haiku translation able to stand on its own.

We agree with Makoto Ueda about the format of a haiku in translation, using the style of three lines with neither a capital at the beginning nor a period at the end, with as little punctuation as possible. For haiku is not a sentence, but rather a fleeting yet eternal moment captured in only a few words. In addition, we have not kept to seventeen syllables because English is a stressed language, unlike Japanese, which is syllabic; therefore haiku which use English syllabic counts often sound contrived. Nor have we used any artificial rhyme or metrical beat—we have merely tried to render the haiku into everyday speech rhythms, and let the English rhythm parallel the Japanese sound if possible.

We have also tried to retain the original line order and order of images, as translators Donald Keene and Edith Schiffert have both suggested. Because Japanese syntax is in inverse order to that of English, to maintain the original order of poetic images it was sometimes necessary to invert lines in English. Although it felt awkward at times, it conveyed the poet's original revelation as she intended. To do our research and translations, we used original sources, especially those compiled by Jodo Nakamoto, a scholar devoted to Chiyo-ni. Our ultimate focus in translation was the presentation of the haiku moment—whether an "ah!" or a greeting or a mere sketch—as simply as possible, like Chiyo-ni breathing her haiku. We hope that at least some of our translations give breath to the original.

We are grateful for the inspiration other poet-translators and co-translators of Japanese poetry have given us, including Kenneth Rexroth and Ikuko Atsumi, Lucien Stryk, Edith Schiffert and Yuki Sawa, William J. Higginson, Sam Hamill, Sanford Goldstein and Seishi Shinoda, and Jane Hirshfield and Mariko Aratani.

As a poet steeped in East Asian culture and meditation for many years, I became interested in translating haiku, and believe that co-translations offer the deepest rendering of the original. I want to express my gratitude to Yoshie, my co-translator. This book could only have been born through a predestined collaboration. Chiyo-ni's spirit was surely with us the whole time and transformed this book as well as our lives. We can only hope that through this book, Chiyo-ni's "haiku moments" may in some way bid others, as well, to stop and appreciate each and every moment of their everyday lives.

—Patricia Donegan

CO-TRANSLATOR'S NOTE

There were several threads in my early life, inherited from my family, which led me to the path of haiku. The first came from my adopted grandfather, who was a creative artist in his everyday life and enjoyed copying haiku on his hand-made pottery cups. As a child, I remember his salon-like house filled with creative people; his younger brother was Kenkichi Yamamoto, who later became a modern haiku critic. Although I didn't really know Kenkichi at that time, in recent years, while translating haiku I have built a new relationship to him through his books on haiku. Another thread was the cultural influence of my mother's family, whose members all practiced some form of art, whether traditional Japanese or modern. Another was my father's overseas work, which gave me a chance to live in Paris and Taiwan, sparking my interest in foreign languages and translation.

Although I later worked for some years as a translator for various institutions, both public and private, I took an unconventional path to becoming a researcher and translator of haiku. I never actively studied haiku until I had a chance to do translation work for Patricia Donegan in Seishi Yamaguchi's haiku classes in Osaka twelve years ago; it was my rare good fortune to become suddenly immersed in haiku study with a master. Curiosity led me further into the haiku world. First, it was my appreciation for the beauty of language, in this case, Japanese poetic words, which magnetized me; in fact, ever since I was a child I enjoyed reading the *saijiki* (Japanese seasonal reference books). Plus, my natural curiosity about people, their life stories and passion for their art, brought me to translating haiku. It was Chiyo-ni's way of life and her devotion to her art that first attracted me. And Pat's coming from America initially on her own to study haiku with a master, and her desire to publish a book about this neglected woman poet, intrigued me. Her devotion to haiku and meditative perspective widened my view of haiku, and her intuitive sense of translation made me understand why Caroline Yang, the former director of the Fulbright program in Japan, called Pat a poet-translator who may well be this generation's Kenneth Rexroth.

My understanding of haiku translation was further deepened by the experience of our writing haiku together informally and in formal monthly all-day *renku* writing sessions. The more we translated and wrote haiku, the more I felt that it was Chiyo-ni's spirit that brought this collaboration about. I feel honored to be the co-translator, and I am grateful to Pat for drawing me into this haiku world. Who knows, perhaps others who read our book will also be gently swept into the path of haiku.

—Yoshie lshibashi

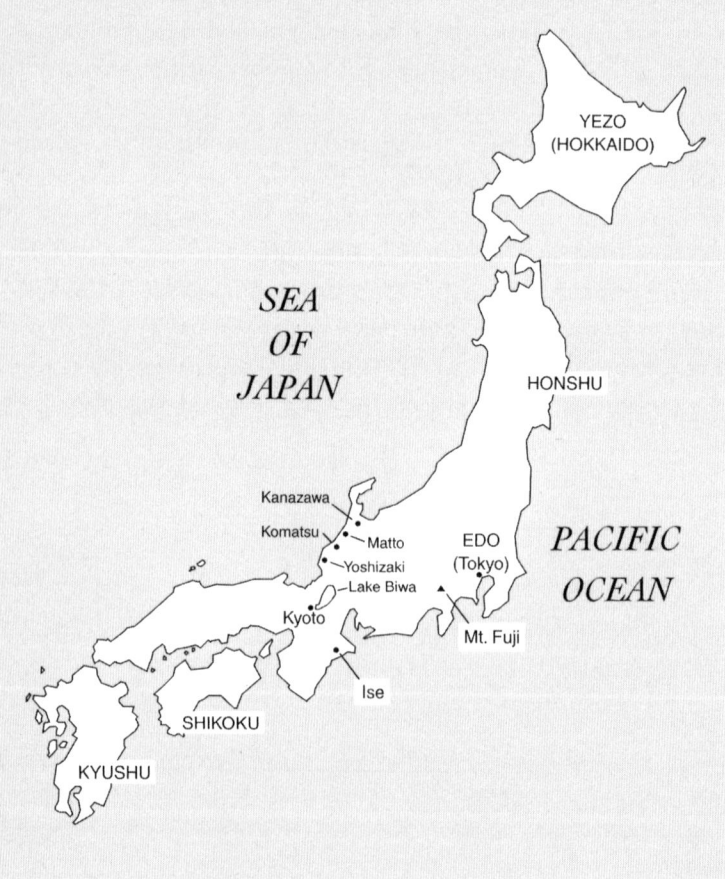

CHIYO-NI'S WORLD
of 18th-Century Japan

YEZO
(HOKKAIDO)

SEA
OF
JAPAN

HONSHU

Kanazawa

Komatsu

Matto

EDO
(Tokyo)

PACIFIC

Yoshizaki

OCEAN

Lake Biwa

Kyoto

Mt. Fuji

Ise

SHIKOKU

KYUSHU

CHIYO-NI'S LIFE

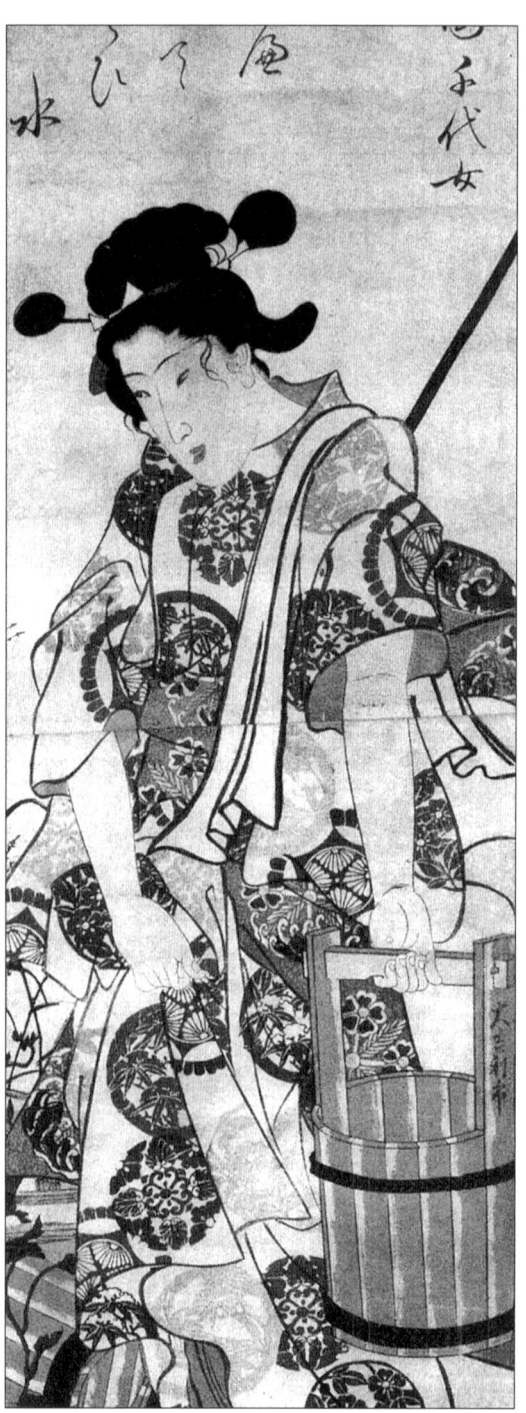

An ukiyoe woodblock print, *Kaga no Kuni Chiyo-jo* (Chiyo-jo of Kaga Province), by Utagawa Kuniyoshi (1798–1861). Keisei Aoki collection. Hakusan, Ishikawa Prefecture, Japan.

morning glory—
the well-bucket entangled
I ask for water

Basho and Chiyo-ni: when thinking of famous haiku poets these two names have always been in the forefront. Among the men there is Basho; among the women there is Chiyo-ni.[1] Japan's most famous woman haiku poet, also known as Chiyo-jo, Kaga no Chiyo, and Matto no Chiyo (Chiyo of the Matto Area), exemplifies the best of the women poets of the Edo period (1603–1867). She is most widely known for her morning-glory haiku above, familiar to most Japanese. Her life is full of legend, yet two things are certain. She lived the Way of Haikai, appreciating each moment, creating art as part of everyday life because she was open to her world. And she achieved fame during her lifetime through her intense devotion to her art in an age when women's freedom and creativity were restricted.

BIRTH AND EARLY LIFE

Chiyo-ni's given birthname was not Chiyo-ni but "Chiyo," meaning "a thousand years"; the feminine suffix "jo" was added, so she was sometimes called "Chiyo-jo" until she changed her name to "Chiyo-ni," when she added the suffix "ni" (nun). However, like many poets in Japan, she used many pen names in her lifetime.

Note: "Chiyo-ni's Life" and "Chiyo-ni's Haiku" were written by Patricia Donegan and researched by Yoshie Ishibashi.

Macrons are used on common Japanese terms in the text and also in the romanized portion of the poetry sections.

Chiyo-ni was born with a writing brush in her hand and with the scent of ink and poetry in the air. Since her family ran a scroll-making business, the local haiku poets and artists would come to have their work mounted by the Fukumasuya family. Because Chiyo-ni became acquainted with poetry, calligraphy, and painting at a very early age, poetry naturally became and remained the focal point for her whole life.

She was born in 1703 in the small town of Matto in the Kaga region (Ishikawa Prefecture), at the foot of Haku-san, or White Mountain, the source of her hometown's sweet spring water. Both Matto and the nearby larger city of Kanazawa were rich in agriculture, the cultural arts, and politics—Matto was governed by one of the most powerful daimyo in Japan's history, the Maeda family. Matto was a well-traveled place; the Hokkoku-kaido (North Country Road) ran right through the middle of town, leading to the old capital of Kyoto in a ten-day walk. So it was a natural stop, a town of many inns, for traveling daimyo and samurai as well as ordinary people and poets like Basho, who took this road on his famed trip, which inspired his *Oku no Hosomichi* (Narrow Road to the Deep North).

Being so far north, the town had very harsh winters, making its residents more acutely aware of the seasonal changes. This helped to sharpen Chiyo-ni's keen powers of observation of nature. Also, because her parents' house was located close to a Buddhist temple, she was born with the ringing of the temple bell in her ears. This environment influenced her vision of haiku and perhaps even led her to later become a Buddhist nun.

At the time of her birth, Matto was governed by the fifth Tokugawa shogun, Tsunayoshi, and fermenting with politics. It was around the time of the legendary samurai story of the Forty-Seven Ronin, who committed suicide together. Yet, the middle Edo period was mostly a time of peace and isolation from the rest of the world; a time of feudal rule but also of a rising working and merchant class; and a time when most of the arts became popularized and flourished in the "floating world," especially the early stages of the colorful ukiyoe woodblock prints, kabuki theater, and the writing of haiku. This rise of urbanized society encouraged the publication of books and the spread of literacy. Literacy was high in Kyoto and Edo (Tokyo), where people pursued literature and the arts, so haiku became popular—books on haiku were second in popularity only to Buddhist texts. Print runs were limited to around three hundred copies since they used carved woodblocks due to the Japanese fondness for calligraphy. It has been estimated that in the early eighteenth century perhaps one adult in twenty may have been able to compose at least a simple haiku.[2]

Information about Chiyo-ni's gifted childhood is incomplete, but she purportedly composed her first haiku at age six.[3] In an early moment of heightened awareness, when she was throwing rice chaff into the stream of her garden, she suddenly saw the beauty of the flowers: "in my garden / star flowers bloom / come and see!" Another account describes Chiyo at age seven, stopping in the midst of playing with her friends in a rice field to gaze up at the geese in the autumn sky: "the first wild geese / coming … / still coming."

When Chiyo-ni was twelve years old, her father, recognizing her talent, sent her to Hansui (1684–1775), a haiku master, to work as his servant for a few years. This was a common practice of the merchant class. He wanted not only to encourage her poetic talent but also to have her learn Chinese characters and the writing of poetry, useful talents for the family's scroll-mounting business.[4] During the Edo period, only about a tenth of the girls, compared to half of the boys, were educated in schools outside the home, yet education was higher for females of the merchant class[5]—so Chiyo-ni was well-educated for her time. She possibly served other families, and learned about literature and haiku from them as well. One of these families, the Sogoyas, a saké-brewing family, had a daughter Suejo, who became a lifelong friend of Chiyo-ni's, as well as her disciple in later years.

Ironically, the most famous anecdote about her, involving the haiku master Rogembo (1688–1747), has been dismissed as fiction because she didn't meet him until she was twenty-five, and not, as alleged, at sixteen.[6] It is the story of her awakening while writing on the cuckoo or nightingale, a theme assigned to her by Rogembo. The story goes that he had rejected her first attempts as contrived. Although the night grew late and the master fell asleep, Chiyo-ni continued musing on the theme until the temple bell rang and he woke to find her still sitting in contemplation. He asked, "Is it dawn?" startling Chiyo-ni, who spontaneously replied with her so-called "enlightenment" haiku: "repeating / *hototogisu, hototogisu*– / the day dawned."

Hototogisu is the Japanese onomatopoeia for a cuckoo's call. According to the legend, Rogembo declared: "This is the haiku I hoped you would make, because it is the genuine expression of your true experience. If you continue like this, you will be a great haiku master."[7]

ENTERING THE HAIKU WORLD

Chiyo-ni was born into a flourishing haiku world. There were many *haijin*, or haiku poets, living in her Kaga-Matto area who had had contact with Basho, such as Hokushi (d. 1718) and Manshi Ikoma, both of Kanazawa, and Kunen Hasegawa of Matto. Although Chiyo-ni was born nine years after Basho died, his influence was still strongly felt, and many of his disciples still preached the Way of Haikai. One famous disciple, Shiko Kagami (1665–1731), became one of Chiyo-ni's main haiku teachers. In 1719, after hearing of Chiyo-ni's creative genius, Chikaku of Kanazawa brought Shiko to her. At that first meeting, when Shiko stayed overnight at Chiyo-ni's house, he asked her to write haiku on two topics: lightning and the iris. For the iris she wrote "spring / remains / in the iris." Shiko also wrote a haiku for Chiyo-ni as he looked at the flower arrangement in her family's *tokonoma* (alcove): "no regret / to use the hibiscus's shadow / as a rain shelter." After she was discovered by Shiko, her name soon became known in literary circles.

Her haiku were published for the first time when she was nineteen, when the poet Rosen (1661–1743) came to visit Kanazawa and held a haiku meeting. Later a haiku anthology, *Hokkoku Buri*, was published in 1722 as a result of his journey to that region, and her haiku "the snowy pond / invites the ducks / to play in the open spaces" was included.

Shiko was so impressed by her that he wrote to a friend that he had discovered a beautiful young woman who had only started writing haiku a year before, but who was already a *meijin* (expert).[8] Although Shiko helped make Chiyo-ni famous, some critics speculate that if Chiyo-ni had not been discovered by Shiko, she might have had an even higher standing as a haiku master, because Shiko had a controversial reputation.[9] She only met him once and mainly kept in touch with him through letters, asking him to correct her haiku. When he died in 1731, she wrote this haiku for him: "sad, so sad / to miss the plum flower / before it fell."

Yet, because of her broad vision and independent mind, over the years she studied with other haiku teachers as well, to develop her own unique style.

Besides being known for her haiku, Chiyo-ni was known for her beauty, which was mentioned by many and recorded in the postscript to one of her poetry collections: "Because Chiyo-ni was such a beautiful young woman, like the wisteria flower [*fuji musume*—a traditional image of a beautiful woman in a kimono holding a sprig of wisteria over her shoulder, used in art and literature], that's also why her name was known all over the country."[10] Another poet, Rokyu, wrote this haiku for Chiyo-ni in 1727: "don't make the traveler / fall off his horse / beautiful grass." A 1740 book of essays quotes the poet Otogo as saying,

"Chiyo-ni was known for her beauty." (One account, however, describes her as plain and overweight; yet, this fails to explain why so many other poets praised her beauty.)[11]

COMING OF AGE: BECOMING KNOWN

It is unclear whether Chiyo-ni ever married.[12] In her day a woman was expected to marry; if she didn't marry, some of the reports of her married life were probably meant to explain some of her haiku which show experience with romance. Volume two of the classic source book of the Edo period, *Zoku Kinsei Kijinden* (Famous People of Edo), cites a possible marriage during the one- or two-year period she lived in Kanazawa, around her eighteenth year, to Yahachi Fukuoka, of the lower samurai class.[13] But both her baby and husband allegedly died soon afterward. Since there is no proof that she married or had a child, however, her two well-known haiku about a child are said to be wrongly attributed to her: "dragon-fly hunter / how far / has he gone today?" and "without the child / who tore the shoji screen / the coldness"; as is the haiku about marriage, "whether astringent / I don't know / the first persimmon picking." [14]

After her husband died, according to one version, the Fukuoka family tried to persuade her to marry his younger brother, as was the custom, but Chiyo-ni refused with this haiku which reveals both her sensitivity and strong will: [15] "what a hot day– / not even the field's rouge flowers / are beautiful to me."

Until she was twenty, haiku was a hobby for her, but after she returned to her parents' home in Matto, she immersed herself in haiku.[16] Yet, while she was living in Kanazawa, she met the editor who published her first haiku, and she also met the haiku poets Shisenjo and Ki-in, who became lifelong friends. Surely in her era, had she been married all her life, she would not have been able to devote herself to haiku as intensely as she did.

Chiyo-ni was unusual for her time, connected with many

male poets and teachers, as well as other women poets. Not long after returning to her hometown, at age twenty-three (and again at age twenty-seven), she made a pilgrimage to Kyoto and Ise to meet and later correspond with haiku master Otsuyu Bakurinsha (1675–1739), a disciple of Basho's disciple Ryoto, of the "Ise countryside style." Otsuyu had, in fact, met Basho when the latter visited Ise, but he was not as close to Basho as Shiko, Chiyo-ni's first teacher, was. Otsuyu was a respected haiku master but had a wild side, frequenting prostitutes of the entertainment district. Although Chiyo-ni was a beautiful young woman, they maintained a strictly teacher-student relationship.[17] Chiyo-ni met Otsuyu only twice, but kept up a longstanding correspondence.

Once, when they met by chance in Kyoto, Otsuyu wrote this haiku for her: "the lily walks by / in a one-layered kimono / Kyoto." They also wrote *renku* together; in one opening verse by Otsuyu, about Chiyo-ni, he depicts her beauty as a traveler: "country name / on her bamboo hat– / fragrant cherry-blossom snow." Otsuyu died in 1739; some years later Chiyo-ni wrote this haiku for him: "loneliness– / felt by the one / hearing the cuckoo." After Otsuyu died, his son Bakuro and disciple Rotai visited Chiyo-ni occasionally, maintaining her connection to her late teacher.

At the time of Otsuyu's death, Chiyo-ni's name became known, and she became very active—making friends with possibly hundreds of haiku poets, and even some samurai artists, who visited her or whom she visited on her literary and spiritual pilgrimages. Since in those days people usually traveled by foot, it was rare to meet as many people as she did.[18] It was also rare that she was able to remain humble even when she became famous, often asking younger poets, some even twenty years her junior, for their critiques of her haiku. She also attended haiku meetings in Kyoto and elsewhere, which was unusual for a woman back then. At one meeting, where she was the only female in attendance (and a country woman, no less) she surprised everyone by writing the best haiku on the full moon: "this evening! / since the crescent moon / I've been waiting." Without even mentioning a full moon it conveyed the strongest impression of moon viewing.

In spite of all this literary activity, Chiyo-ni continued to lead a simple life. One haiku poet, Koko, wrote about Chiyo-ni's humility: "the morning glory– / in this floating world / there is no fence." Chiyo-ni wasn't living in seclusion, since the road to Kyoto ran right in front of her house. She could hear the sounds of the world in her kitchen and the sounds of nature in her garden at the same time. She remained in both worlds. Nor was she seeking fame in the capital of Edo, trying to establish herself as a great haiku master or open a lucrative poetry school, as other poets did. But rather she chose to lead a simple life, not separate—"there is no fence"—from the everyday world of other people or poets high and low.[19]

MID-LIFE

Later, a succession of tragedies occurred while she was in her thirties, when members of her family died, including her parents, brother, and his wife, leaving her alone to carry on the family's scroll-making business. In 1748, when Baiji of Ise visited, and Chiyo-ni composed haiku with twenty other *haijin*, she signed her name as "Matto scroll-maker, Chiyo."[20] Yet, from 1733 to 1743, she couldn't write as many haiku as before because of these misfortunes and her heavy work schedule. She couldn't fully devote herself to haiku again until she was almost fifty, when she adopted her niece, Nao, and Nao's husband Rokubei or Haku-u, to take over the scroll-making business, which was customary at the time. Around the time of her retirement from the business, she wrote this haiku: "bird's song / left to the world / now it's just the sound of the pine." By then many of her teachers and close friends had also died, including Shiko, Otsuyu, and Ki-in, and Chiyo-ni felt bereft. All of these deaths brought her closer to the Buddhist teachings of impermanence, as seen in her later haiku.

Because Chiyo-ni didn't become a nun until age fifty-two, Tsuyu Kawashima, in *Joryu Haijin*, notes that before that time she may have had one or more love affairs.[21] One of her haiku speaks knowingly of the sorrow of separation and waiting for a loved one, in the voice of an old woman or geisha looking back on her life's past loves:[22] "no more waiting / for the evening or the dawn– / touching the old clothes." And perhaps her many haiku (sixteen) about star-crossed lovers written for the Tanabata festival reveal an interest in romance, as in these haiku: "what shadow / can the star lovers meet in / before the moon disappears" and "the reeds / also blossom / when the stars meet." While there is no substantive evidence confirming love relationships, some of her haiku and letters show a closeness to several people. But whether these relationships were platonic, romantic, or familial is uncertain.

Taisui, also known as Hansui, was a male haiku poet nineteen years older than Chiyo-ni. Chiyo-ni lived with Hansui and apprenticed under him for a few years in her adolescence. They lived near each other and in later life they became nun and monk, respectively. Their haiku were published in the same anthologies; they wrote haiku together and for each other; and both died in the same year. They could never have married because he was of the samurai class and she was of the merchant class. Yet, some scholars speculate that Nao was not Chiyo-ni's niece but in fact her daughter by Hansui.[23] For his eightieth birthday Chiyo-ni wrote a haiku which reflects their long and caring relationship: "one more sleep / till one hundred years– / the willow tree."

In another haiku Chiyo-ni expresses rare emotions for the young haiku poet Gosen, who may have been her son by the haiku poet Ki-in:[24] "till his hat / fades into a butterfly / I yearned for him." One haiku that Ki-in wrote for Chiyo-ni is an intimate and sensual portrait: "ivy in the garden / looks shiny / wet with water for her hair.[25] Ki-in died when Chiyo-ni was forty-eight; she may have become a nun to assuage her loss.

The person closest to Chiyo-ni was Suejo. Their letters and haiku suggest something more than strictly a master-disciple relationship, and a familial intimacy unlike the feelings between Chiyo-ni and her other women haiku-poet friends, such as Karyo-ni and Kasenjo.[26] Chiyo-ni and Suejo met almost daily and wrote constantly. They were in the same haiku circle and wrote haiku together and for each other.

Forty of their letters remain. Even though their houses were only minutes apart, if they couldn't meet for even a few days they would write letters instead. These letters were sometimes to exchange haiku and comments on each other's work: "I liked your spring haiku best," and "I'm anxious for you to see my work in the *One Hundred and One Poets' Anthology*—sorry it's taking so long to get a copy to you." Besides their letters the two women also wrote *tanrenga*, or dialogue/short-linked poems. In one, Chiyo-ni begins: "Having been invited to meet Suejo we wrote together: in this lively place / the peony / most beautiful."

To which Suejo replied: "the waning night / the morning moon awaits." These show an intimacy rarely found in their poems to other people.

In later years, when Chiyo-ni was older and ill, Suejo took care of her. When Chiyo-ni died, Suejo wrote these prefaces and haiku:

Having read your last haiku, even though I know it's the nature of the world to die, I still feel grief:

in the shadow
the moon is hidden–
such sorrow

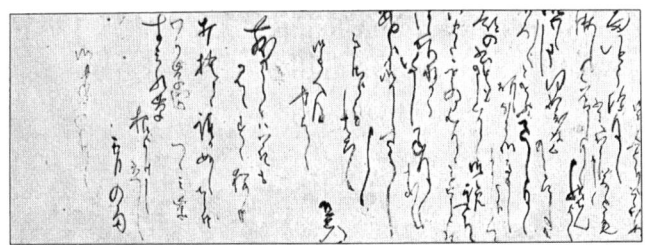

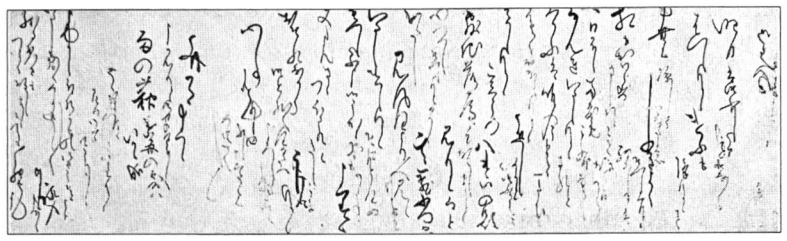

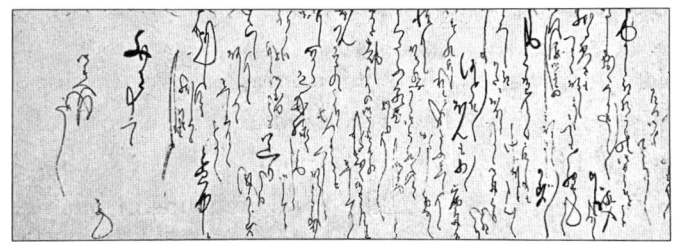

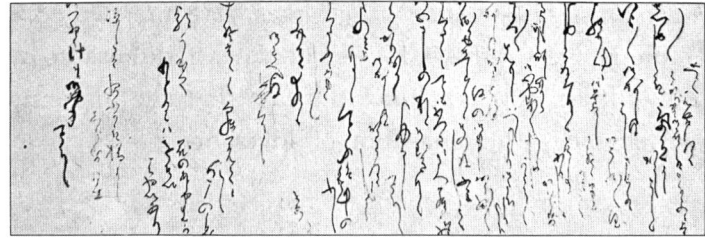

3. Scroll of Chiyo-ni's calligraphed letters to Suejo (1721–90), her female disciple.
Matto City Museum, Matto City, Ishikawa-ken, Japan.

Seven years after Chiyo-ni's death I remember her calligraphy:

> white chrysanthemum's
> unchanged shadow—
> print of the moon

Fifteen years later when Suejo died, Haku-u, Chiyo-ni's adopted son, said: "They were so close; both yearned for the stream of Basho . . . leaving behind many fine haiku." He wrote: "remembrance / in the field / remains of bush clover and pampas grass." Suejo and Chiyo-ni, the bush clover and pampas grass side-by-side—their lives were intertwined.[27]

Ultimately, whether Chiyo-ni actually had these involvements is less important than the fact that she understood impermanence—the separation of loved ones.

CHIYO-NI AS NUN

In 1754, at age fifty-two, Chiyo-ni became a Jodo-Shinshu (Pure Land) Buddhist nun and added the suffix *ni* (nun) to her name, and thereafter was known as Chiyo-ni (Chiyo the nun). Her ordination came rather late in life; other women poets who became nuns, such as Kikusha, did so around age thirty. By then Chiyo-ni was ready to move to a new stage of peace and nonattachment after many years of struggle.[28] In traditional Japanese arts, from the twelfth century on, there were ways or paths (*dō* or *michi*) thought to lead to enlightenment. Among them are *sadō*, the way of tea; *kyūdō*, the way of archery; *shodō*, the way of calligraphy; and *kadō*, the way of poetry (referring to tanka/waka poetry).

Like Basho, who espoused haiku as a Way, or a life's path (*haikai no michi*), and who also wrote his best haiku in his later years after meditating in a Zen temple for ten years, Chiyo-ni's

36

best haiku were written in her later years after becoming a nun and devoting her life to Buddhism and haiku.[29] Yet Chiyo-ni did not live permanently in a temple, as conventional nuns did, but continued to live in her home, enjoying the freedom and respect that the status of a nun gave her, and the rare privilege, as a single woman, to travel and meet other poets, especially male poets, for it was usually forbidden for women to associate with male outsiders. As an artist and a nun, Chiyo-ni was outside the class system and therefore not restricted by the normal social codes imposed upon women, whose activities were usually confined to their homes and governed by male family members,[30] according to the three obediences: when young obey your father, when married your husband, and when widowed and old, your son. In Chiyo-ni's case, her only obedience was to follow the path of Buddhism and haiku.

Even after she became a nun, Chiyo-ni remained exceptionally active. She wrote haiku with prostitutes, socialized with male and female poets, created collaborative art with samurai, wrote haiku as gifts for foreign envoys, published two poetry books, traveled and wrote haiku on the road, and celebrated everyday life outside the temple. Her self-portrait (Fig. 26) also shows her in the pose of *uta-hiza*—one knee up on which to write a haiku on a *tanzaku* strip of paper. This captures her identity as both poet and nun.

It was quite common in Chiyo-ni's day for talented women to choose the life of a Buddhist nun, as much for its spiritual calling as for the freedom it gave them as women to create their art and to travel and associate with other artists in ways they could never have done as ordinary, restricted women in the society of eighteenth-century Japan. The biographies of women haiku poets of the Edo period attest that many lived as widows, Buddhist nuns, or prostitutes; these roles may seem at odds, but each gave women the freedom they needed as writers. It was a common custom in East Asia for ex-prostitutes to become nuns in their old age, since there has been less of a moral stigma attached to this profession there than in the West. A nun like Chiyo-ni had several close prostitute poet friends, Kasenjo (who also became a nun in her later life) and Oku, whom she visited and wrote poetry with as well.

The Jodo-Shinshu sect of Buddhism was founded in the thirteenth century by Shinran, espousing a simple faith in Amida Buddha (Buddha of infinite light and compassion) and using the recitation of *nembutsu* prayer as the way to salvation and enlightenment and rebirth in the Pure Land. This opened Buddhism up to lay people who couldn't handle the rigors of Zen monasticism. Jodo-Shinshu was often called the "easy gate," and in Chiyo-ni's day it was the most conventional form of Buddhism.

For her ordination, Chiyo-ni took the Buddhist name Soen (Simple Garden), and sometimes signed her haiku and paintings thus. On the day she had her head shaved, she wrote the following preface and haiku:

> I am not rejecting the world, but because of feeling a lonely sense of *mujō* [impermanence] I am rather seeking a way for my heart to take after pure water, which flows night and day.

> putting up my hair
> no more—
> my hands in the *kotatsu*

Some say this is one of Chiyo-ni's *satori* (enlightenment) haiku.[31] Here the *kotatsu* (a quilt-covered table with a charcoal brazier under it) reflects her calm state of mind. She continued to live an ordinary life, but her heart was not ordinary; it was devoted to the spiritual path of haiku.[32]

Perhaps it was the influence of Buddhism which kept her humble and uninterested in creating a Chiyo-ni school of haiku, devoted rather to the spirit of haiku even in the midst of her public life and ever-increasing fame. One male *haijin* friend, Mafu, wrote this haiku for her ordination: "how elegant / barely touching the mirror– / winter moon." Here Chiyo-ni is depicted as the winter moon, detached from her ego and the world's reflections. Suejo wrote this haiku for her: "ink-dyed kimono / now you can play / with the moon and flowers," meaning in nun's clothes she could dedicate herself to the path of haiku.

From her childhood Chiyo-ni enjoyed hearing the teachings of Buddhism at the local temples, listening to the monks' stories; later they provided solace after the deaths in her family. Recognizing that all human beings have sorrows, Jodo-Shinshu emphasized the light of compassion for all living things. It was through Buddhism that she learned compassion, to let go of her self-centeredness and become empty, like grass blown in the wind.[33] As she wrote in one haiku: "anyway / leave it to the wind / pampas grass." Jodo-Shinshu's emphasis on boundless compassion surely influenced Chiyo-ni's haiku, which shows her tenderness for and identification with other creatures and phenomena, such as the following: "soaring skylark– / what do you think / of the limitless sky" and "dying sweetfish– / day by day / the river harsher."

When she was twenty-four Chiyo-ni composed her famous gourd haiku, which she painted many times and included as one of her favorite poems in various anthologies. On her visit to a Zen temple, Eiheiji, the abbot had asked her to write a haiku on the Buddhist theme *sankai* (the Three Realms): desire, form, and nonform. She responded spontaneously: "a hundred gourds / from the heart / of one vine." The Zen master was surprised by the young poet's enlightened understanding that everything arises from the mind (Fig. 21).

Although Chiyo-ni lived as a nun very much in the world, living in her own house rather than in a temple, between 1754 and 1758, according to John M. Rosenfield, she may have entered Sainen-in temple in Kanazawa for religious training, as there are few haiku preserved from that period.[34] There is one about a nun's temple: "nuns' temple / feast for the women / the sound of crickets." Another describes a *rohatsu* (eight-day silent meditation retreat): "even / the flowing water / doesn't say anything."

Yet some say that Chiyo-ni, like most *haijin*, probably never practiced formal meditation. Master Nakano, the current abbot of Shokoji temple in Matto, whose father, the previous abbot, wrote a book on Chiyo-ni, comments:

> In the Jodo-Shinshu tradition there is no formal meditation as in Zen, but her haiku was a meditation, and all her haiku written after she became a nun were enlightened haiku. . . . Before she became a nun, she had too much technique, trying to impress people, but after becoming a nun, she was liberated and purer and forgot herself. She saw things as they were, which is the so-called "ah!" moment, or *ichi-go-ichi-eh* (appreciation of this moment's one meeting). As seen in her following haiku:
>
> > full moon
> > keeping it in my eyes
> > on a distance walk
>
> The moon is a symbol of realization. This haiku shows she has no attachments, walking on the spiritual path, relaxing in the light of the moon, which cools desire, and keeping the light of awareness in her eyes.[35]

It was this haiku which Chiyo-ni chose to write in calligraphy on her *zutabukuro*, the cloth bag which she wore as part of her Buddhist robes.

The basic tenet of Buddhism, that of *mujō*, or impermanence, is naturally reflected in most haiku, Chiyo-ni's as well.

This follows Basho's edict on the importance of becoming one with nature and capturing its fleeting quality. Although all cultures have an awareness of the mutability of life, in Japanese culture there is language for it that is both artistic and religious. *Mujō* embodies people's thinking and is an aesthetic term pervading the poetry as well. Perhaps the cataclysmic nature of the Japanese archipelago—with its earthquakes, tidal waves, and volcanic eruptions—made people more acutely aware of the passing of things. This awareness became a natural part of haiku, in a poignant way. Haiku, which usually refers to nature, depicts it not as "fallen," as in the West, but transient; there is an acceptance and appreciation of its evanescence. In Japanese aesthetics this is called *aware*, or sad beauty. Observe the following: "traces of a dream / a butterfly / through the flower field" and "clear water is cool / fireflies vanish– / there's nothing more" and "among a field / of horsetail weeds– / temple ruins."

Besides *mujō, mushin*, another Buddhist term referring to a mind that is empty, pure and open, is evident in Chiyo-ni's haiku, as the following: "green grass– / between, between the blades / the color of the water" and "sounds enter the water / on this night– / *hototogisu*" and "the autumn wind / resounds in the mountain– / voice of the bell." As one of her contemporaries noted: "Her style is pure, like white jade."[36]

Another quality of her writing is clarity. Her images are precise and luminous, and often evoke clear water. In the Jodo-Shinshu sect there is a practice called *suisōkan*, contemplation of water,[37] to produce compassion in one's ordinary, nonmeditative state of mind. Whether Chiyo-ni did this kind of contemplation isn't known. But *shimizu*, or clear water, was a significant symbol for her; it originated in the sweet spring drinking water of her hometown and was one of her most frequently used images. She declared: "I want my heart to take after pure water." Just as the moon's reflection in the water traditionally symbolizes Zen enlightenment, so clear water can suggest the sharp, precise clear reflectiveness of mirrorlike wisdom[38] and clear vision, yet at the same time simplicity, since water is a most common yet precious element. This clarity is apparent in her following haiku: "clear water: / no front / no back." Here she captures the coexistence of all phenomena: the good, bad, happy, sad. And the haiku below vividly expresses the heightened awareness that comes when the mind is attentive to the moment: "rouge lips / forgotten– / clear springwater." This clarity of mind is also apparent in her death haiku, as scholar Nakamoto notes:

> Her death haiku shows her calm mind, like a Zen master's, shows how pure her mind was, like a clear-blue autumn sky. Till the last moment she loved nature and died peacefully surrounded by friends; magnetizing others to her open mind.[39]

"I also saw the moon / as for this world– / ah–goodbye." The moon represents the appreciation of the phenomenal world as well as enlightenment and compassion. The last line is like the letting go—with a long last breath—in acceptance of this fragile, transient world.

CHIYO-NI AS ARTIST

Traditionally in East Asia the "three perfections" of calligraphy, painting, and poetry were considered *one* art, and Chiyo-ni excelled in all. For the Japanese, the visual/spatial effect of calligraphy is almost as important as the meaning. Haiku is usually calligraphed in one vertical line, but sometimes for visual effect in two or three lines, as Chiyo-ni did in some of her paintings. (Fig. 9).

Because she was born into a family who mounted other artists' and poets' works on *kakejiku*, or hanging scrolls, Chiyo-ni was steeped in the arts from an early age. She was a largely self-taught painter, like most *haijin* of the time, yet an innately talented one.[40] Since there were many famous artists living in her area and around Kyoto, like the painters Taiga Ike and Gyokuran Ike, who collaborated with Chiyo-ni (Fig. 24), she was naturally influenced by their art. She also did receive some formal training. One calligraphy teacher, Genemon Yamamoto (1656–1725) from Kanazawa, of the *jimyōin* school of calligraphy, taught a somewhat heavy masculine style, but Chiyo-ni's calligraphy lines are usually seen as more feminine, refined, and freer than this traditional style.[41] Nobutaka Aoki, an art collector and literati from Matto who owns some of Chiyo-ni's original calligraphy, observes that her cursive style, with its soft and energetic lines, is impossible to imitate, as some people have tried to do. Her unique calligraphic style can be divided into three periods: early period, with a light, playful style; middle, with a delicate, subtle style; and late, with a simple, Zenlike style.[42]

Chiyo-ni purportedly studied painting with three teachers: Shunmei Go (1699–1781) of the Kano style; Shijoken Yada (1719–94), a painter and former samurai from Kanazawa, of the Hasegawa style; and Hyakusen Sakaki (1697–1753) of Nagoya, a *haijin* disciple of Otsuyu and painter, also of the Kano style. Hyakusen is said to have influenced the great *haijin* painter Yosa Buson (1716–83), who lived during this period.[43] Even though Chiyo-ni studied painting formally, her style has a freshness and spontaneity of composition, and her masterly use of space is intuitive.[44] Although Chiyo-ni has an image as a nun, her artistic style reflects strength and spontaneity.[45]

Traditionally in East Asia, it is common for a painter and poet to collaborate. Besides their spiritual and aesthetic dimensions, art and poetry have always had a social function in Japan, rather than being only solitary work. There is nothing quite comparable in the West to the collaborative, spontaneous literary and artistic activity in Japan. Chiyo-ni is a good example of a person who often did collaborative art with her poet-artist friends as well as samurai artists, such as Toho Naito, whenever

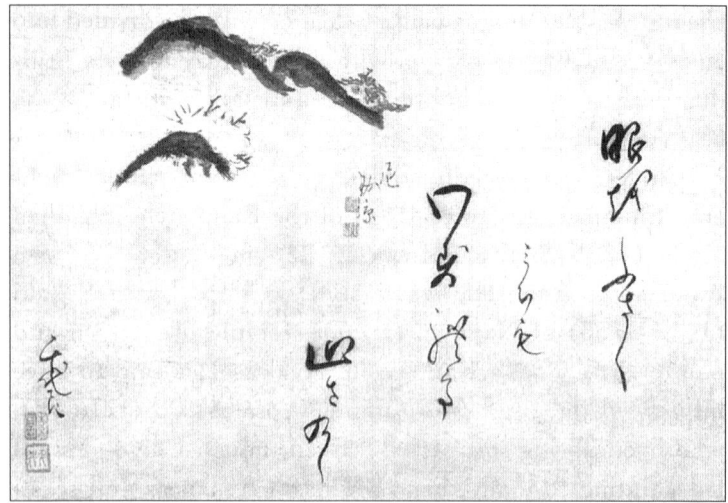

4. A *haiga* with Chiyo-ni's calligraphy, done in her later years, of her cherry-blossom haiku, *me o fusagu / michi mo wasurete / yama-zakura* (eyes oblivious / to the path— / mountain cherry blossoms), illustrated by her female haijin friend Karyo-ni. Matto City Museum.

they visited. They would create occasional haiku and paintings or write linked verses, such as this painting and haiku by Chiyo-ni and her woman poet-painter friend Karyo-ni. (See Fig. 4).

As well as collaborations, Chiyo-ni continued to do her own work, but even these were dialogues with real occasions—say, of attending a temple memorial service and noticing a butterfly: "Buddhist service– / the butterfly too / voiceless." This image could easily be put into a painting. Haiku poets like Chiyo-ni often combined both the haiku and the painted illustration of the haiku on the same paper, which was known as a *haiga*, or a haiku painting. Through the presentation of an image, her paintings heightened the *kigo*, or seasonal element, essential to haiku, reaching into the *hon-i*, heart of things, evoking the emotional meaning associated with each season, like the image of the cricket evoking the lonely feeling of autumn. Because Chiyo-ni was such a fine painter of *haiga*, her haiku became even more known and cherished, something that everyone wanted to hang in their *tokonoma* (alcove). She often gave these as gifts to her friends and other *haijin*, and was often asked by others to paint something on the spot. Painting and writing spontaneously were among her everyday activities.

Besides *haiga*, Chiyo-ni painted portraits, including her own. One important portrait of hers, one of the two that have been documented, was included in a collection of thirty-six famous *haijin*'s haiku and portraits entitled *Seshu Meiroku Hokku-Shu*, published by Chomu in Kyoto in 1770. It was a portrait of Chigetsu (1632–1706), the most prominent woman disciple of Basho and in her day, a *haijin* as famous as, or more famous than, Chiyo-ni.[46] This one painting is significant because it attests to and celebrates the continuing lineage of women haiku poets and artists.

WOMEN POETS OF THE EDO PERIOD

There is a strong tradition of female poets in Japan, dating from the Heian period (784–1185), when Murasaki Shikibu wrote *The Tale of Genji*, the world's first novel, and women began to dominate tanka court poetry, which became the accepted form for women writers. However, later in the seventeenth century, when haiku took hold, it was thought to be mostly a male form since it was seen as more objective, less emotionally direct than the earlier tanka form, and thus "unsuitable" for women.[47] Moreover, there was the rigid suppression of women's rights during the Edo period, which added to the difficulty of becoming a writer. Against these odds, women haiku poets flourished. In the Edo period after Basho's death (1694–1867) there were at least three hundred women haiku poets actively writing.[48] Some women before that time studied with Basho directly and some, like Chiyo-ni, later studied with his disciples.

Women *haijin* are mentioned in such books as *Kokin Haikai*

Onna Kasen (Women Haikai Poets of Modern and Ancient Times), written and illustrated by the famous artist Saikaku Ihara in 1684, and *Mikawa Komachi*, published by a disciple of Basho in 1702, which includes haiku by sixty-seven women poets. In 1774, at Buson's request, Chiyo-ni wrote the foreword to the 1774 *Haikai Tamamoshu* (Seaweed Haiku Collection), a collection of haiku by women poets who lived before Chiyo-ni, including disciples of Basho such as Chigetsu and Sonojo. Another women's anthology was published in Chiyo-ni's time, the *Himenoshiki* (The Princess Ceremony) in 1726, including *hokku* and *renku* by Chiyo-ni and others. These *renku* are among the few remaining linked verse (36 links) written in collaboration by two women haiku poets.

However, because women haiku poets were not usually taken as seriously as the men, records of their haiku and their biographies are scarce, except in cases like Chiyo-ni, who was too famous to be ignored. In order for women to be acknowledged they had to outshine the men. Chiyo-ni's talent and fame let her mingle freely in the male *haijin* world, but her women poet-friends were vital to her. Women gathered to write haiku because it was difficult to attend male haiku meetings. Although Chiyo-ni attended male gatherings sometimes, it was unusual, and she usually met male *haijin* in informal settings. Ironically, although haiku began as a movement toward a more egalitarian poetry, it largely excluded women. While Basho had some women disciples, eventually the "seventeen rules of Basho" pervaded, which forbade male haiku poets from befriending female haiku poets (in later years the "seventeen rules" were said to have been wrongly attributed to Basho).[49] On the whole, women couldn't enter the haiku world on their own, but had to enter through their husband, father or male relative; even after entering the haiku world, it was almost impossible to be regarded as an equal.[50]

Today, ironically, the majority of practicing haiku poets in

Japan are women. Chiyo-ni and her peers led the way; some were prominent in the haiku world, some less so, but all were dedicated to the path of poetry and to each other.

CHIYO-NI'S WOMEN POET FRIENDS

There are four women poets who were especially close to Chiyo-ni: Suejo, Kasenjo, Shisenjo, and Karyo-ni. Suejo (1721–90) was Chiyo-ni's main disciple and closest companion. They knew each other from Suejo's childhood. Later Suejo married Shi-ho (1715–81) who was also a *haijin*, of the Ise style. All three were close, yet Chiyo-ni and Suejo became closer after Suejo, at the age of thirty-two, began writing haiku and studying with Chiyo-ni. Although Suejo was eighteen years younger than Chiyo-ni, her mentor, they nurtured and depended upon each other. They wrote haiku and *renku* together and were in the same circle of poet friends. One example of their *tanrenga*, or short linked poem, begins with a preface and opening by Chiyo-ni:

During *Hinamatsuri* [the Doll Festival] we enjoyed dipping the calligraphy brush in the peach flower saké and wrote:

> dawn's
> parting
> unknown to dolls

to which Suejo replied: "opened shoji screen– / the fragrance / of the bird's shadow." Because Suejo was a disciple of Chiyo-ni, she received instant recognition, and her poems were included in several anthologies. Kihaku, the editor of Chiyo-ni's books, put several of Suejo's haiku in his anthology *Yaburegasa* (The Torn Hat) with this praise: "Suejo learned *fūga* [the Way of Elegance or Haikai] from Chiyo-ni and therefore acquired Basho's *shofū* [style]."[51] Suejo also had one book of haiku published, *Hotosha* (Peach Cave House), in her lifetime.

The second woman poet close to Chiyo-ni was Kasenjo (1703 or 1715–76) who was from Mikuni, in Fukui Prefecture. In her younger days she was a prostitute and went by the name Hasegawa, but in her later years she became a nun like Chiyo-ni, naming herself Takitani-ni (Waterfall Valley). Because Chiyo-ni was also a strong woman she could sympathize with Kasenjo's way of life, so they were close.[52] It wasn't unusual for a nun to be friends with a prostitute because both were outside the normal social structure, having freedom unlike other women to devote to writing. Denjo, a woman haiku poet from the Edo period, wrote a haiku for Chiyo-ni and Kasenjo: "please shine / Chiyo-ni of Kaga, Kasenjo of Echizen / two night moons." On one of Kasenjo's visits in 1774, a year before Chiyo-ni died, Chiyo-ni wrote this greeting haiku for her friend: "the old days / beautifully in bloom– / the winter peony."

Some of Kasenjo's haiku and some of her *renku* are included in the *Himenoshiki*. Other prostitute friends of Chiyo-ni's were also included in this collection: Oku Michiko, Kaoru, and Wakamurasaki. Kasenjo also had her life documented, along with Chiyo-ni's, in the book *Zoku Kinsei Kijinden* (Famous People of the Edo Period), published in 1798. Kasenjo left behind a death poem, as was the custom: "at the bottom / how cold / the sound of the sea," which shows a deep sadness as well as a sense of *aware*.

Another woman poet close to Chiyo-ni was Shisenjo (dates unknown) of Kanazawa, the wife of *haijin* Yaka-ku. In later life she also became a nun and took the name So-shin-ni. She was reportedly older than Chiyo-ni. The two composed *renku* together. Shisenjo said that they both "have poles in the same river of haiku." Their two most famous *renku*, along with some of Shisenjo's *hokku*, were published in the *Himenoshiki*. These *renku* were written in 1725 when Chiyo-ni, aged twenty-four, visited Shisenjo's house, and they decided to dedicate their *renku* to Gyozenji temple, a women's temple for the safe delivery of babies.

Karyo-ni (1696–1771), another woman poet close to Chiyo-ni, was also from nearby Kanazawa. She was the disciple of Ki-in (who was the disciple of Shiko). In later life she also became a Buddhist nun. There is record of a gathering with Kasenjo, Chiyo-ni, and other *haijin* friends who came to celebrate, to mark the occasion by writing haiku and *renku* together.[53] In 1761 they took a rare and long trip together to Kyoto. There remains one *haiga* of theirs—Karyo-ni's illustration of Chiyo-ni's haiku about the mountain cherry blossoms (Fig. 4, p. 44). There are also two of their dialogue haiku calligraphed on a bamboo hat and towel: "just a glimpse of / flowers on the road / Yoshino mountain" (Chiyo-ni) and "only traces / of sunlight / the grassy flowers" (Karyo-ni).

Another woman poet who was likely connected to Chiyo-ni was Shokyu-ni (1713–81), another well-known woman *haijin* from Kyushu, whose teacher was Yaha, a disciple of Basho. After her husband's death, she also became a nun. It is certain that Suejo and her husband, as well as some other mutual friends of Chiyo-ni's, met Shokyu-ni in Kyoto, since there is Suejo's record of letters and haiku exchange, so Chiyo-ni must have at least known about her, if not met her in person.

The lineage of Chiyo-ni and her peers continued and still continues to bloom in the following generations of women-haiku poets who traveled and are still traveling the path of haiku.

LATER LIFE

The latter part of Chiyo-ni's life was her most active period in the haiku world. She published two collections of her poetry in her lifetime, which was rare for any poet, but especially for a woman, and her poems were included in more than 120 anthologies. She was acquainted with most of the literary and artistic luminaries of her time, as well as statesmen. In 1763, at the age of sixty-one, she had the honor of being commissioned by the Lord Maeda of Kaga to inscribe twenty-one of her poems in calligraphy on scrolls and fans, which were included among gifts from the Tokugawa government to Korean envoys. She was also asked by other poets, like Buson, to write forewords to other poetry collections. Although she was not directly involved in the Basho revival, led by Buson in Kyoto, she was a colleague of younger haiku poets in the Kaga area like Ranko and Bakusui, who were active participants.

Besides the many well-known poet friends that she often visited and wrote haiku and *renku* with, she had at least one main female and one lesser male disciple who studied with her, namely Suejo (1721–90) and Chiseki (1735–84), respectively.

As she grew older, Chiyo-ni's health suffered, especially in the last five years of her life, and she was often bedridden and cared for by her close haiku friends, especially Suejo. Yet she still continued composing haiku. One reveals her failing health: "my energy / can only defeat a butterfly / this spring morning." She left behind several death poems, written not long before she died in 1775, at the age of seventy-two. Among them is: "clear water is cool / fireflies vanish– / there's nothing more." As news of her death spread, many haiku expressing grief poured in; all alluded to her gentleness and greatness as a haiku master. Chomu (1731–95), a famous *haijin*, eulogized: "how to look at this world / without losing the way / winter moon." Her adopted son Haku-u wrote in a letter to Chomu informing him of Chiyo-ni's death: "We have lost the light of the haiku path."

Years after Chiyo-ni's death other women *haijin* came to Matto to pay their respects. In 1781, one well-known poet and artist, Kikusha (1753–1826), visited Chiyo-ni's grave and spoke to Haku-u, whereupon she was moved to write the following haiku: "the cherry blossoms / that are revealed to the heart— /

please sway."[54]

During her life and after, many myths arose about Chiyo-ni's life and haiku. Some haiku by other poets have been wrongly attributed to her, such as the famous mosquito-net haiku, supposedly written by the prostitute Ukihashi: "whether getting up or lying down / how large / the mosquito net."[55] Anecdotes such as the "cuckoo enlightenment" story are said to be fiction.[56] Unfortunately, people tend to focus on the legends and her few well-known haiku, and overlook her finest work.[57]

She left behind 1,700 haiku that we know of, in haiku notebooks, calligraphy on *tanzaku*, screens, and fans; in letters; in some *haibun* (combination of prose and haiku, usually written as travel diaries); and many on her *haiga* paintings. After her death, memorial sites were built at temples including Senkoji temple in Kanazawa and Shokoji temple in Matto. All claim to have Chiyo-ni's grave. Shokoji has a museum of her artwork and some personal effects, such as her walking stick, bamboo hat, and writing brush, a Chiyo-ni-do (Chiyo-ni Hall), and her grave site where one of her death poems is inscribed on a *kuhi* (poem stone).

Even after her death her poetry remained popular. Chiyo-ni's image has been depicted in various forms such as paintings, statues, songs, a Noh play, a traditional Japanese dance, playing cards, saké labels, and even cookies. Most importantly, she was often depicted in paintings of groups of famous poets, and in the later Edo period she was depicted in the *ukiyoe* woodblock prints of artists Utamaro's, Toyokuni's, and Kuniyoshi's series of famous women. In Kuniyoshi's (1797–1861) woodcut of Chiyo-ni (see Frontispiece), she is shown surrounded by morning glories, symbolizing both her most famous haiku and her life of simplicity, living the Way of Haikai. Her haiku survive not only because they were memorable or well-known in their time, but because her way of life appealed to people.[58]

CHIYO-NI'S HAIKU

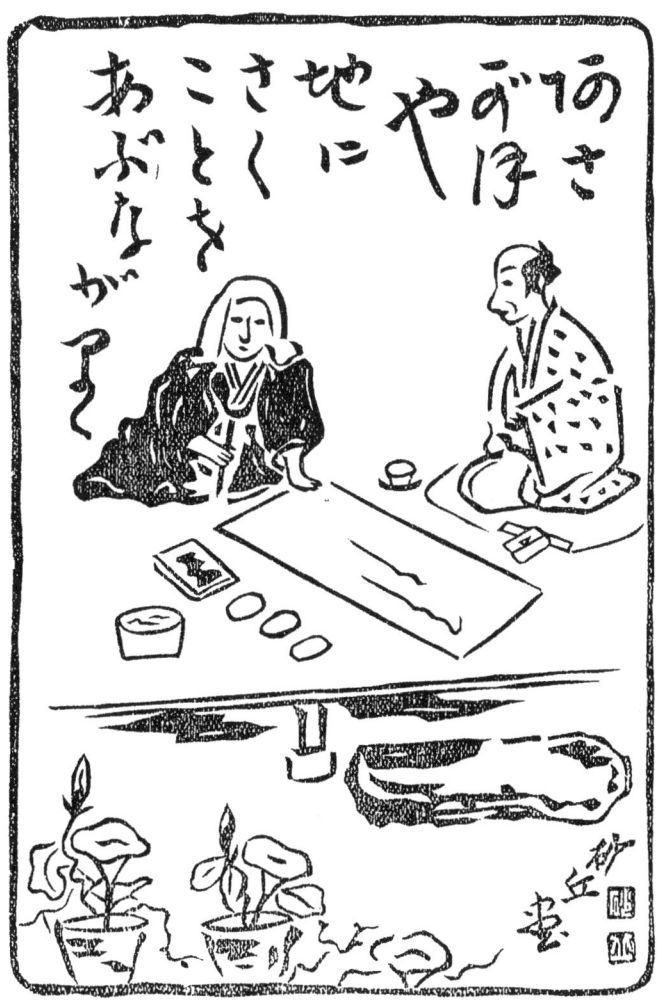

5. A woodblock print by Sakyu Komatsu depicting Chiyo-ni writing a morning glory haiku. From *Chiyo-ni no Issho* (The Life of Chiyo-ni), by Jodo Nakamoto; published privately in 1935, on the occasion of Chiyo-ni's 150th memorial, by Kinen Kyosankai, Matto City.

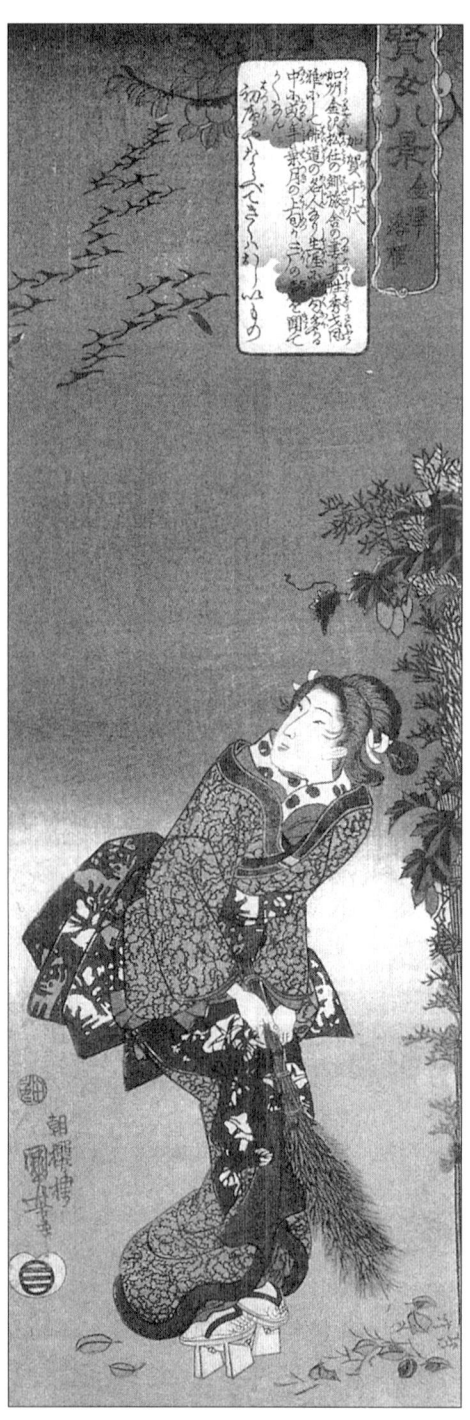

6. An ukiyoe woodblock print (ca. 1843–45), *Geese Alighting on Kanazawa: Kaga no Chiyo*, by Utagawa Kuniyoshi (1798–1861), from the series "Eight Reflections of Virtuous Women." Raymond A. Bidwell Collection, Springfield Museum of Fine Arts.

THE HAIKU FORM

Haiku is now the most popular and well-known poetic form in the world. Containing only seventeen syllables in three phrases (5-7-5) in Japanese, or three lines in English, a fine haiku usually presents a crystalline moment of heightened awareness in simple imagery, traditionally using a *kigo*, or seasonal reference from nature. The *kigo* most likely has shaman/Shinto roots, for tanka poetry, the precursor to haiku, has its origins in spells and chants to evoke the deities.[1] Haiku is a way to call the spirit of the thing named, whether it be the spring rain or full moon. *Kigo* are a kind of shorthand; the emotions (personal/societal) attached to seasonal words make explanation unnecessary. For example, the words "autumn wind" evoke a lonely feeling.

Originally, the seasonal words came from the farming and fishing people who lived intimately with the seasons, rather than from a literary elite. Later, these *kigo*, based upon centuries of tradition and consensus, were compiled in seasonal reference books called *saijiki*, which most Japanese haiku poets still use today. Contemporary haiku poet Kristin Deming comments: "The use of *kigo* is a way to enter the heart of the poem quickly, because it tells the season, the mood, and the cultural associations with only one word."

The Japanese language, unique in its abundance of standard *kigo*, has subtle poetic descriptions for natural images which don't exist in English or other languages. For example, there are more than forty *kigo* for the moon alone, such as hazy moon, spring moon, star moon night, emerging moon, hesitant moon, frozen moon, dawn moon, and more. However, the beauty of the *kigo* is that no matter what language haiku is written in, this insistence on a seasonal reference makes one connect to the natural world outside the self, and relate to this moment, this time, this place. As the late woman *haijin* Teijo Nakamura noted: "Today's wind is today's wind; today's flower is today's flower."[2]

In the tradition of Basho, objectivity (*kyakkan byōsha*),[3] or what can be termed "objective heart," epitomizes the approach and method: "the heart"—a fleeting perception deeply felt; "the objective"—the perception expressed through concrete imagery with little or no comment. Because of its brevity and the suggestive nature of the Japanese language itself, haiku relies upon suggestion. And while most poetry in the world uses suggestion, it is the essence of the haiku form. To create a powerful haiku, a contrast of the eternal and the immediate present is often used, for in order to become aware of the eternal there must be some momentary perception.[4] There need to be two electric poles between which a spark leaps for the haiku to be effective; otherwise it is just a brief statement.[5]

These two elements are usually divided by a break called a *kireji*, or cutting word, like *ya*, *keri*, or *kana*. A dash is often used as the division in English. Moreover, in Japanese there are emotional overtones of emphasis attached to these *kireji* which are untranslatable. These two elements (the eternal and momentary) can be easily seen in Chiyo-ni's haiku: "but for their voices / the herons would disappear– / this morning's snow." Here the snow is the eternal aspect of nature, and the cry of the herons, the fleeting moment. In another haiku of hers: "rouged lips / forgotten– / clear spring water" the water represents the eternal, and the makeup on her lips the momentary perception. These are moments when one's breath is literally taken away, upon seeing something with clarity when the mind is open and not crowded by thoughts. As *haijin* Kazuo Sato explains: "Haiku is a poetry of 'ah-ness' because it makes you say, 'Ah, now I see.'"

This meditative and objective approach to haiku is most known in the West, having been introduced by R. H. Blyth, D. T. Suzuki, and others in the stream of Zen Buddhism. But to search for the "Zen mystery" in every haiku is a mistake; to do so would take away their personal, subjective flavor. Objectivity in haiku has been often overemphasized in the West. Often Japanese warn against the limits of looking at haiku from only a Zen perspective, saying that haiku is much more ordinary. This "ordinariness" resonates with the Buddhist idea of *mujō*, which is a natural part of haiku's expression, that is not necessarily Zen, but a poignant way of looking at the world, in appreciation of each fleeting moment.

For example, haiku is often just a "sketch" of fleeting nature, an approach which was first espoused by Basho and later called *shasei* by modern haiku poet Shiki. As in these haiku of Chiyo-ni's: "the shimmering haze / above / the wet stone" and "above / the mirage / mountains of clouds." Yet it is important to note that some modern haiku poets have advocated using "the sketch" in combination with reflections from the mind, such as Seishi Yamaguchi's "imagination jump" or Yatsuka Ishihara's "introspective shaping."

HAIKU AS GREETING

Haiku are usually not categorized in Japan. The most common function of haiku has always been *aisatsu*, or greeting—a way to open oneself and connect with another person or thing in nature. It is very social: a simple recording of an appreciated moment usually between two people, as in this haiku Chiyo-ni wrote for a visiting friend: "just for now / I spread the morning's snow / over the dust" and one for a departing friend: "if only I could tie / the string of my kite / to the hem of your kimono." Usually these haiku as greetings were given to the visiting person as a gift, and sometimes the person replied with a greeting haiku as well. This understanding of haiku as a social activity is important, because it takes haiku out of the realm of mystery into its natural realm of the everyday.

Since haiku was traditionally meant to be a greeting or dialogue with the world and nature, rather than writing carefully and revising in solitude, spontaneity is important. Of course it is true that Chiyo-ni sometimes wrote by herself and revised her work, making different versions of the same moment (for example, the four or five versions of her "rouged lips forgotten" haiku). Yet spontaneity was always deemed important to capture the original, fresh moment. Even Basho said there shouldn't be a breath's hesitation between the perception and the writing of what is perceived.[6] Likewise, Chiyo-ni often wrote spontaneously in social settings, as was the custom for haiku poets. There are many stories of Chiyo-ni writing haiku on the spot. One story is when Lord Maeda of Kaga asked her to write a poem as he was passing by the street.

She responded: "looking up / at the plum blossoms– / the frog." Spontaneous greetings made haiku a greater part of everyday life.

This spirit of *aisatsu*, on the whole, has been lost to modern times, with poets writing more objective, individualistic "art" haiku, which is more of a monologue than an engaged dialogue with the world. Kenkichi Yamamoto, a modern haiku critic, stressed that haiku originally had a dialogue aspect, of an unspoken tag question (using a haiku of Chiyo-ni's as an example, "the silence / of the moon / enters the heart [doesn't it?]"). In the deepest sense of the word, haiku is a greeting, because haiku, originating from the linked-verse form written between two or more persons, demanded a greeting: an attention to *mugen*, or the eternal moment, to connect or link the next verse, to the other person, to nature, to whatever was present in the environment.[7] The first verse, or *hokku*, of the linked poem had to be a greeting or toast, to the people present, marking the occasion, season, mood, and so on. Later the *hokku* were written as independent poems, and became haiku. And even though haiku may be about nature (*yuki, tsuki, hana*: snow, moon, and flowers) rather than people, it still embodies the heart and spirit of *aisatsu*.[8] In Chiyo-ni's time, the greeting aspect of haiku was highly revered.

POETRY, POLITICS, AND THE BASHO REVIVAL

Before his death in 1694, Basho transformed haiku into a poetic form of depth and sophistication. After his passing, the form tended to revert to its older character as either trite or amusing wordplay, except for gifted poets like Chiyo-ni.[9] Following Basho's death, his school fragmented into factions; after his disciples died it got worse. Donald Keene notes: "Yet even in the worst period of *haikai*, a few poets preserved something of the tradition of Basho. The rustic schools of Mino and Ise . . . rather than the poets of Edo, eventually paved the way for a revival of *haikai* poetry—Kaga no Chiyo-jo deserves special mention among the rustic poets."[10]

The rustic school was led by Kagami Shiko (1665–1731), one of Basho's ten main disciples[11] and one of Chiyo-ni's teachers. Shiko, a haiku theorist, emphasized Basho's theory of *karumi*, or lightness and simplicity: to make haiku simple, to include the bare essentials of what is really there, to take subjects from daily life so everyone can understand, and to make haiku a way of life,[12] as recorded in his book, *Kuzu no Matsubara* (Pine Grove of Kuzu, 1692). In the last three years of his life, Basho told his disciples to rid their minds of technique and superficiality by means of *karumi*—like looking at a shallow sand-bed river, the beauty of things plain and ordinary, as opposed to colorful, ornate beauty.[13]

Basho regards one of his haiku in particular as an exemplar of *karumi*: "bush warbler– / droppings on a rice cake / left on the porch." This aesthetic is very delicate, often misunderstood, and difficult to master, for one has to present the moment's simplicity without being overly simple or banal, or writing what the Japanese term as "*tsukinami* haiku"—haiku that are too common.

Sometimes poets associated with the rustic school, including Chiyo-ni, have been criticized for this, but perhaps critics miss her subtle style. And undoubtedly even the greatest of masters wrote more *tsukinami* haiku than great ones.

Although many of Basho's disciples resisted this late theory,[14] others, like Shiko, followed it to extremes. When Shiko was young he resided at a Zen temple for ten years. Later, when he was twenty-six, he met Basho when Basho was forty-seven, and accompanied the poet on his last journey to Matsushima. Shiko specialized in explaining Basho's theories and coedited the *Sarumino* (Monkey's Raincoat, 1698), as well as the *Oi Nikki* (Diary of the Book Satchel, 1695). Supposedly Basho was fond of Shiko, and when Basho was dying he dictated his will to the younger man, calling him trustworthy and giving him his favorite Buddhist statue.[15]

Later, the famous *haijin* Buson Yosa (1716–83), who headed the rival school of haiku, labeled Shiko a "peasant-style Basho," and other poets similarly disdained him. Although Shiko helped to popularize haiku throughout the country, some accused him of falsifying Basho's theories in order to lend greater authority to his own ideas and attract his own following. Yet in his theories Basho's basic ideas still resonated.[16] On the one hand, Shiko popularized haiku and took it to the common people; on the other hand, in order to make haiku theory understandable he had to oversimplify it, which offended the poets of the Edo school of haiku.

Chiyo-ni was fortunate to study with several teachers, such as Shiko, who were direct disciples of Basho; yet some say it is regrettable that Chiyo-ni was not discovered by someone other than Shiko, because she was so talented.[17] Some say it was also unfortunate that Chiyo-ni was born a few years too late to study directly with Basho. Since she was such an exceptionally talented, intelligent woman, likened to Sei Shonagon, author of the *Pillow Book*,[18] she might have developed her talent further.

Since Chiyo-ni was linked to the Mino-Ise countryside school through her teachers Shiko and Otsuyu Bakurinsha, and to a lesser degree Hansui, or Taisui and Rogembo, both successors to Shiko, she was thrust into the midst of poetry politics. Yet because of her intelligence and humble personality she remained independent, following her own style, publishing her haiku in many different schools' anthologies, and connecting with poets of various lineages.[19] Some of these other younger poets were involved in the Basho revival led by Buson in Kyoto, like Ranko (1726–98), who wrote the forewords and afterword to Chiyo-ni's poetry collections, and Bakusui (1718–83), who was an early student of Ki-in's.

The Basho revival began around 1743, the fiftieth anniversary of Basho's death. According to Buson, the revival was a return to Basho's original ideas and a departure from any of the trends which downgraded haiku. This was more than a decade after Shiko had died, yet the target was still the countryside school, which was said to oversimplify or vulgarize haiku, making it too common.[20]

Although Chiyo-ni was caught up in the delicate politics, she remained widely respected. Although Buson criticized Chiyo-ni, along with her friend Kasenjo, in an essay—"in Kaetsu there are famous women haiku poets, but their haiku is weak and emotional because it is women's haiku"[21]—he couldn't ignore her,[22] and even asked her to write the foreword to his *Haikai Tamamoshu* poetry collection. Buson's main disciple, Kito, a close friend of Chiyo-ni's adopted son, wrote a mourning haiku for her when she died, demonstrating the respect she commanded from other poets.

THE HEALING POWER OF HAIKU

In Japan there are many beliefs in the power of poetry—Chiyo-ni's included. Words are believed to have spirit or power, as in the word *kotodama* (*koto*, "word"; *tama*, "spirit"), for the language of the gods and goddesses. And originally, as in most cultures, Japanese poems in ancient times were religious incantations. As noted previously, tanka poetry, the precursor to haiku, evolved from shaman chants believed to have the power to move the gods and demons. In the Edo period and even today haiku poets have maintained that haiku has unusual healing powers and helps to prolong life.

There are several stories about the powers invested in Chiyo-ni's haiku. According to one, the governor of Kaga had heard about Chiyo-ni's fame and once asked her to write haiku as gifts for some Korean envoys. Later, when he needed her to revive his garden's most beautiful cherry tree, which was ailing, he invited her to the palace. There she spontaneously composed this haiku: "spring will come again— / without flowers / you'll be firewood." To no one's surprise, the tree began to bloom again.

CHIYO-NI'S POETRY COLLECTIONS AND DISCIPLES

Chiyo-ni published two collections of her poetry in her lifetime, which was unusual for any poet, especially for a woman, in the Edo period. In 1764 when she was sixty-two *Chiyo-ni Kushu* (Haiku Collection of Chiyo, the Nun) with 546 haiku was published; and in 1771 when she was sixty-nine *Haikai Matsu no Koe* (Haiku: Voice of the Pine) with 327 haiku was published. She also wrote a preface for a *saijiki* (seasonal reference book) of that period, as well as forewords to six poetry collections, including Buson Yosa's *Haikai Tamamoshu* (1774), which was a great honor.

Remarkably, Chiyo-ni's poems were included in more than one hundred poetry anthologies while she was alive, and some twenty more after her death. Her teacher Shiko even included her poems in his prestigious haiku anthology. She also had the honor of being one of ten women poets included in the *Haikai*

Hyakuichi-shū (One Hundred and One Haiku Poets' Collection) of 1765, in which each poet had one representative haiku and a woodblock portrait (see Fig. 20, p. 162); this collection was very popular in Chiyo-ni's time.

As well as her haiku poetry, she also wrote many *renga* (linked verse) with others; many examples remain, including the well-known *Himenoshiki* (The Princess Ceremony, 1726). Of her *haibun*, only one short example remains which we know of, although she probably wrote several, which was customary. The extant *haibun*, *Yoshizaki Mōde* (Pilgrimage to Yoshizaki), was written in 1762 when she was around sixty years old.

Although there is no record that she set up a school of haiku or wrote about her theories, she did have several disciples. Her most important disciple was Suejo (1721–90) There are names of two other women disciples, but no definitive information.[23] She also had a lesser male disciple, Chiseki (1735–84) from Takayama, who supposedly studied with her, although he is not included in all the haiku "lineage trees."

Chiyo-ni's prolific publications and haiku disciples attest to her greatness and her stature as a poet during her lifetime.

CHIYO-NI'S HAIKU STYLE

In her day it was said that Chiyo-ni's style was true to Basho's. Although Chiyo-ni acquired her own unique voice eventually, she was surely influenced in her early period by the prevalence of Basho's teachings in the Kaga region. Ranko, author of the afterword to *Chiyo-ni Kushu*, wrote that Kihaku, the editor, had originally decided to collect Chiyo-ni's haiku because she was true to Basho's *shofū*, or style.[24] Basho's style of haiku was formulated by others over the years. His well-known fundamentals usually include: *sabi* (detached loneliness), *wabi* (poverty of spirit), *hosomi* (slenderness, sparseness), *shiori* (tenderness), *sokkyō* (spontaneity), *makoto* (sincerity), *fūga* (elegance), *karumi*

63

(simplicity), *kyakkan byōsha* (objectivity) and *shizen to hitotsu ni naru* (oneness with nature).

"Oneness with nature" seems especially resonant in Chiyo-ni's haiku. Basho's theory of oneness with nature was that the poet should make a faithful or honest sketch of nature. In the *Sanzoshi* (1702), Basho's disciple Doho explains his teacher's theory: "Learn about the pine from the pine and the bamboo from the bamboo—the poet should detach his mind from self . . . and enter into the object . . . so the poem forms itself when poet and object become one."[25] This experience is analogous to the Buddhist idea of *satori*, or enlightenment, what Kenneth Yasuda called the "haiku moment."[26] When writing haiku Chiyo-ni immersed herself in nature, honestly observing what she saw, as in the following haiku: "sound of things / dropping from the tree– / autumn wind" and "a single spider's thread / ties the duckweed / to the shore."[27]

Roughly ninety percent of her haiku are about things in nature rather than the social realm. This kind of haiku practice emphasizing seeing things clearly, becoming one with nature, and living the Way of Haikai co-emerged with her Buddhist practice.

Purity and clarity, as noted previously in the discussion of "Chiyo-ni as Nun," are central to Chiyo-ni's poetry. The haiku poet Shoin, who wrote the preface to *Chiyo-ni Kushu*, stated:

Chiyo-ni's style is pure, like white jade, without ornament, without carving, natural. Both her life and her writing style are clear/pure. She lives simply, as if with a stone for a pillow, and spring water to brush her teeth. She is like a small pine, embodying a female style that is subtle, fresh, and beautiful. Chiyo-ni knows the Way, is in harmony with Nature. One can better know the universe through each thing in phenomena, as in Chiyo-ni's haiku, than through books.[28]

Her clear writing style went hand in hand with her Buddhist

practice. In her haiku, water can be a symbol for clear percep-
tion. She saw the world clearly and expressed her words clearly,
using the image of water, one of her most frequently used im-
ages (thirty-five "clear water" haiku versus ninety-three "cherry
blossom" haiku, for example), to reflect nature. For example:
"hands drop / all things on the ground– / the clear water" and
"on the road / today's rain / the seed for clear water." And this
haiku, perhaps more than any other, epitomizes her clear per-
ception: "when dropped / it is only water / rouge flower dew."

Yet, the most important thing about Chiyo-ni's haiku, which
epitomizes her being true to Basho's style, is how she actually
lived the Way of Haikai, or *fūga no michi* (the way of refinement
in one's life and art). With the emphasis on poetry as a way of
life, poetry could be a source of awakening. One famous Edo
story attests to this. Kaya Shirao (1738–91), an arrogant young
male poet, visited Chiyo-ni for the first time when she was six-
ty-seven, and wept after meeting such a great haiku poet who
was so humble, living the Way of Haikai. Although she never
set up a "Chiyo-ni school," many people of her time admired
her lifestyle, following the way of haiku, and felt that, "even
though" she was a woman, she shared something in common
with Basho.[29]

CHIYO-NI'S FEMALE IMAGERY

"Chiyo-ni's haiku is pearl-like, while Basho's is diamond-like,"
commented one contemporary woman haiku poet, Suzuko Shi-
nagawa.[30] A pearl can be characterized as sensual and delicate.
However, this kind of subjective and subtle style in Chiyo-ni's
time, as well as now, is often marginalized if not as objective and
precise as male writing. Often women poets' haiku are praised
not for their feminine style but for their masculine style exclud-
ing any subjective elements.[31]

While it is true that many of the haiku written by Chiyo-ni

and other women *haijin* are universal and don't reflect any par-ticular gender perspective in either form or content, many of her poems do reflect a sensuality of feeling and imagery not usually found in male haiku. Others reflect an unusual sensitivity to the images of women of her period. Some embody an almost imper-ceptible delicacy of imagery which could be labeled as feminine. And all show a careful observation of the details of everyday life more often honored by women.

Much of Chiyo-ni's imagery has a sensual, pearl-like qual-ity—dew swollen on buds, rouged lips, a woman' naked skin, rouged fingertips on a white chrysanthemum, a change of kimo-no, moonflowers sleeping as lovers, the peach-white skin of chil-dren, the loneliness of sleeping alone, or catching a cool breeze in one's kimono sleeves. One such haiku, "change of kimono: / showing only her back / to the blossom's fragrance" has a subtle sensuality, and a reticence that is unusual because it's not simply about being shy to a lover, although that is implied, but being shy even to the fragrance of the blossoms wafting in the air.

In the haiku "moonflowers– / when a woman's skin / is re-vealed" the white moonflower, which only blooms in the eve-ning twilight, heightens the beauty of the contrast between the skin's whiteness and the dark. The moonflower is also an allusion to the name of a lover of the prince in *The Tale of Genji*.

Another example of a sensual haiku is: "eventually / whose skin will they touch– / rouge flowers" see note on p. 126. The rouge makeup for the lips was traditionally made from the saf-flower; the poet looks at the beauty of the flowers and wonders whose skin they will touch someday in another form, what woman will put the rouge to her lips. While there is an appreci-ation here of the tactile, there is also a sense of *mono no aware*, the beauty of passing things. Beauty fades, as does the flower; yet for a moment it is vivid, sensual, and red.

The willow is another sensual image, traditionally regarded as beautiful and feminine in shape—the shape associated with hair, eyebrows, and hips. Chiyo-ni used the willow image in approximately forty haiku, including the following: "to tangle / or untangle a willow– / depends on the wind."

She also often used the image of the butterfly, which is a traditional symbol for a woman, as well. For example: "the butterfly / in front and back / of the woman's path."

Chiyo-ni frequently used imagery which reflects the sentiments and concerns of the women of her times. Emphasis on beauty: the following haiku is perhaps Chiyo-ni's answer to women who were overly concerned with the appearance of their kimonos: "in the moonlight / whatever you wear becomes beautiful / moonviewing." One need not worry, she seems to say; in the soft moonlight, everything appears beautiful. Emphasis on reticence (an important virtue for Japanese women of the times): "the path / of the lily / is to bow her head" and "even moonviewing / women desire / shadows." Emphasis on the everyday tasks of women restricted to their homes: "sewing things– / I fold in dreams / on a December night."

Although the women felt restricted, inwardly they still had their dreams. Another haiku voices a woman's desire to express her feelings more in her confined world: "airing out kimonos / as well as her heart / is never enough." At the same time, she shows her refined sensibilities in her preparations for an arriving guest: "just for now / I spread the morning snow / over the dust."

Chiyo-ni often wrote about small things in nature, using imagery as delicate and subtle as mist in the air—the moonflower in candlelight, fireflies at dusk, a dream of spring blossoms, purple cremation smoke compared to the iris flower, and the light on white tea flowers. As in the following haiku: "what would moonflowers / look like / in candlelight?" and "the moon's shadow / also pauses– / cherry blossom dawn."

Yet, Chiyo-ni's haiku sometimes displayed her strength of character as well, a boldness of style in contrast to her more delicate haiku, as seen in the following: "how terrifying / her rouged fingers / against the white chrysanthemums" and "woman's desire / deeply rooted– / the wild violets" and "butterfly / you also get mad / some days."

It is interesting to note that as Basho grew older, he became more open to the simplicity of everyday life and arrived at his last haiku theory of *karumi*, or simplicity. Traditionally, and especially in Edo Japan, women did not have the male privilege of expanding their horizons, so their truth or spirituality was often found in the mundane. Women tend to validate daily life and recognize that miracles exist within the mundane, which is the core of haiku. Yet contemporary women's haiku about small things are sometimes still dismissed as "kitchen haiku"—as if there were something less valid about careful observation of the everyday. Chiyo-ni was a master at making connections, by being open and carefully observing the ordinary things around her, especially in nature. Her observation was simple and clear, yet at the same time unique, with its feminine imagery that was delicate and sensual. The most important thing to her was honoring the sacredness of everyday life.

LITERARY CRITICISM OF CHIYO-NI'S HAIKU

Chiyo-ni's morning-glory haiku (p. 152) is her most famous and controversial. Most Japanese, at least those in their middle age, may not remember her name but know this haiku. Yet its reception has been mixed: it has been characterized variously as an egotistical poem or an enlightened one. Ironically, Chiyo-ni herself probably didn't think that much of it; she included it in only one of her poetry collections. Although she wrote twenty-eight haiku on this flower, she sometimes saw the humor of it all, as in "morning glory– / the truth is / the flower hates people."

Kyoshi Takahama (1874–1959), a well-known twentieth-century *haijin*, was one of Chiyo-ni's fiercest critics. His criticism of her haiku was initially broadcast on the radio in the 1950s. At that time he admitted that she was an accomplished poet. But he didn't value the haiku poets of her era, including her main teachers, Shiko and Otsuyu, because they were too subjective and downgraded haiku; rather, he only valued haiku poets Basho, Buson, and his teacher Shiki.[32] More specifically, he said that Chiyo-ni, in the morning-glory haiku, should have just observed nature and not have personified it. He felt that she was conceited, showing off her kindness and phony *fūga*, or elegance. It was ridiculous, he declared, to ask a neighbor for water just because she didn't want to break the flower's vine.[33]

Master Nakano, the current abbot of Shokoji temple in Matto, commented:

> Because there are so many stories, people don't know the real Chiyo-ni. If you look into this haiku deeply you can see it as an enlightenment poem. However, some critics have seen it differently; for example, Kyoshi Takahama . . . had a limited view of Chiyo-ni's most famous 'morning-glory' haiku. The little information he had he got from a monk who didn't especially like Chiyo-ni, and he only used this haiku because it was so famous and he could therefore use it as a springboard to criticize other haiku poets of her era.[34]

After Kyoshi's broadcast people wrote letters to protest. He replied that it was necessary to criticize haiku which displayed "wrong tendencies," and expressed irritation that even women and children knew Chiyo-ni's haiku but not Basho's or Buson's.[35] People still continued to enjoy the morning-glory haiku, in spite of Kyoshi's criticism. Yet, because he was such a powerful modern critic, he influenced several generations to ignore Chiyo-ni's worth, so people often do not see beyond this one haiku, to examine her other haiku more deeply.

Also in contrast to Kyoshi are two Buddhist scholars who see

Chiyo-ni's morning-glory haiku as an expression of her enlightenment. First, D. T. Suzuki compares Basho's famous frog poem to Chiyo-ni's "morning-glory" haiku:

Basho's frog produced a sound by jumping into the old pond, and this gave him a chance to commune with the spirit of the old pond—the pond as old as Eternity itself. In Chiyo's case, it was the morning glory that acquainted her with the spirit of beauty. . . . One late summer morning, Chiyo found the bucket entwined by the morning glory vine. . . . She was so deeply struck by its beauty that she forgot her mission. . . . This is a case of perfect identification between subject and object, seer and seen: the whole universe is one flower. . . .[36]

At the time, the poetess was not conscious of herself or of the morning glory standing beside her. Her mind was filled with the flower, the whole world turned into the flower, she was the flower itself. When she regained her consciousness, the only words she could utter were, 'Oh, morning glory,' in which all that she experienced found its vent. . . .[37]

And so the thought never occurred to Chiyo that she should untwine the vine in order to free the bucket for her use; hence she went to the neighbor for water.[38]

The other scholar and Zen master, Aitken Roshi, comments:

Some critics find this poem too precious, but Suzuki points out that one of Chiyo-ni's variants for the version, usually cited, used *ya* rather than *ni* at the end of the first segment. The *ya* serves to cut the verse at that point, and to express the 'ah' experience of the poet, lost in just that morning glory. So Professor Suzuki translates the haiku: 'Oh, morning glory! / The bucket taken captive, / Water begged for.' . . . [This] is the great compassionate heart, to beg for water rather than to disturb the vine.[39]

When evaluating the work of someone famous like Chiyo-ni, it is easy to get lost in legend and only look at the well-known stories and popular haiku, and miss the essence of her work itself. So her haiku has drawn different reviews over the years. It is also hard to know what is the most valid criticism when it differs from century to century. In the Edo period Chiyo-ni's haiku was popular and she was revered as a great haiku poet. Yet while some modern critics think she is a fine haiku poet, other critics undervalue her either because of her association with the Mino school of popularized haiku, or because she was a woman.[40] Ironically, even some modern female scholars criticize her haiku as being too feminine and therefore not artistic enough,[41] a euphemistic way of saying not masculine enough. A few critics even say her haiku might be overestimated because she was one of the rare woman *haijin* of her times. Yet being a woman writer in a male-dominated haiku world was a struggle, not to mention living in eighteenth-century feudal society, which restricted women. If her talent and achievement are seen in this light, it is remarkable that she achieved as much as she did, so her haiku should be even more valued.[42]

Because haiku critics tend to use Basho as a measuring stick, it is impossible to avoid comparisons. Some say the real value of Chiyo-ni's haiku is missed because of her fame, nearly equivalent to Basho's, and because of the tendency of the critics to focus on her famous haiku. Some critics say that while some of her haiku are common, some are as great as Basho's.[43] But what does that really mean? No writer, Basho included, always writes great haiku, and Basho even said: "If one writes a few great haiku in a lifetime, that is enough."

So, one can only read Chiyo-ni and judge for oneself. What matters is that she wrote haiku which were genuine to her, illuminating universal heightened moments of human experience—which bid us to stop for a moment, connect to nature and appreciate our own everyday world. This is the true spirit of haiku—to maintain an appreciation of the moment.

ONE HUNDRED HAIKU

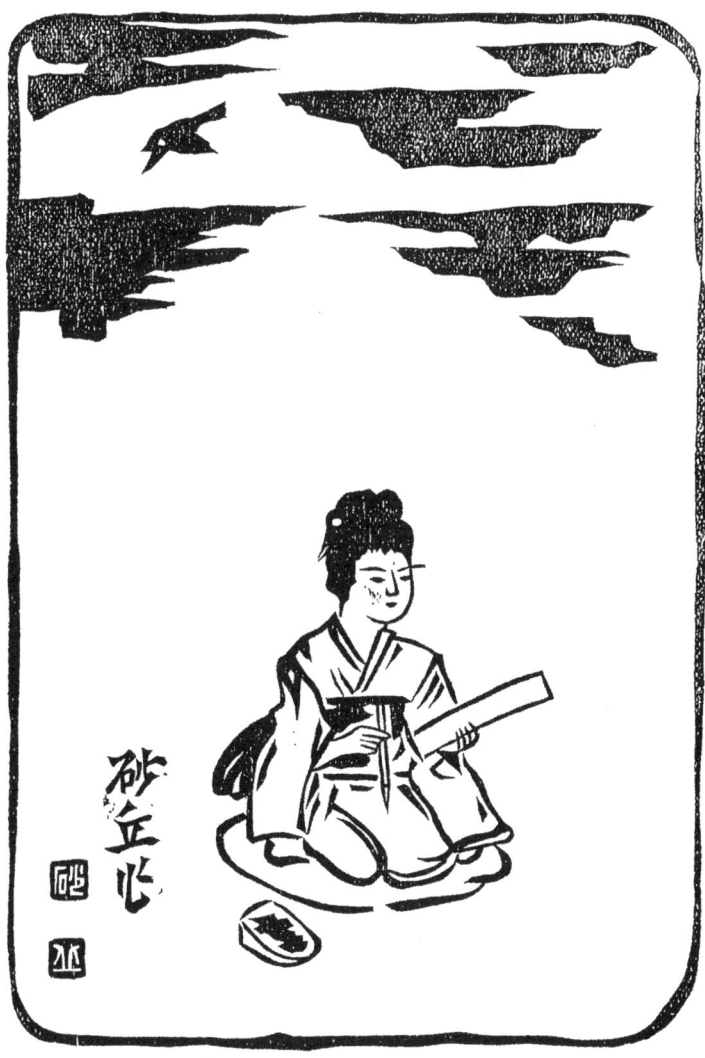

7. A woodblock print by Sakyu Komatsu depicting Chiyo-ni writing her enlightenment haiku on the cuckoo, supposedly at age sixteen. From Nakamoto, *Chiyo-ni no Issho*.

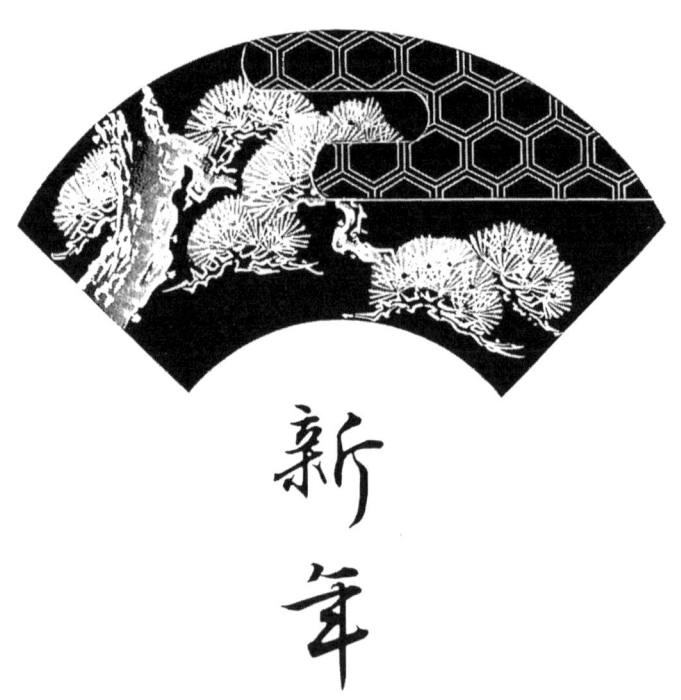

新年

tsuru no asobi
kumoi ni kanau
hatsu hi kana

flying of cranes
as high as the clouds–
first sunrise

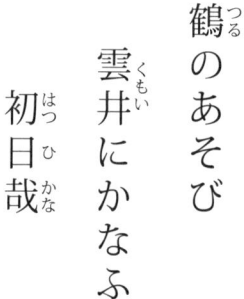

kigo (seasonal reference): *hatsu hi* (first sunrise)

Translators' Note: In this volume, the Japanese characters appear either in vertical columns proceeding from right to left or in horizontal lines which are read from left to right. The vertical style is traditional.

more izuru
yama mata yama ya
hatsu-gasumi

one mountain after another
unveiled–
the first mists

も れ 出る
山 又 山 や
は つ 霞

kigo: hatsu-gasumi (the first mist)

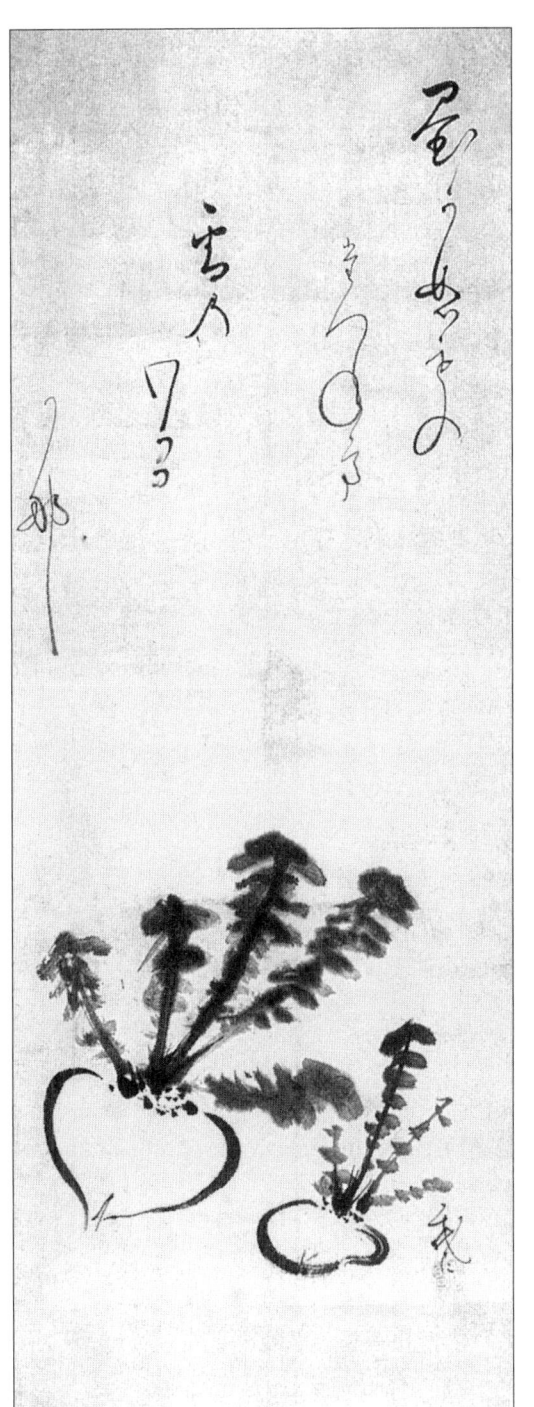

8. A *haiga* by Chiyo-ni at age sixty-five: *okanu mono / tazunete yuki no / wakana kana* (not having planted them / I must search for young greens / in the snow). Matto City Museum.

hito ashi ni
sagi mo kieru ya
wakana no no

so many people
the herons disappear–
fields of seven herbs

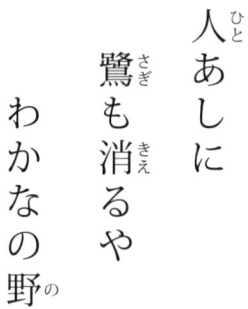

kigo: wakana no no (fields of seven herbs)

Note: Among the traditional New Year's activities of Japanese families is going out on January seventh for the "picking of seven herbs" to make *nana-kusa-gayu* (seven-herb porridge), a food thought to bring good health in the New Year.

Written with joy for my grandson and the peaceful New Year, 1775. *

hatsu-zora ni
te ni toru Fuji no
warai kana

under New Year's sky
holding Mount Fuji's
smile

初空に
手にとる富士の
笑ひ哉

kigo: hatsu-zora (New Year's sky)

Note: Mount Fuji represents her adopted grandson wearing *hakama* (traditional robe) for the ceremony for five-year-old boys. Because Chiyo-ni had been sick with asthma for some years, she especially cherished this joyful moment. She died in the autumn of that year.

*Notes such as these were written by Chiyo-ni on her original manuscripts. Called *maegaki*, these words or phrases record the occasion, place, month and date when the haiku was written.

toso sake ya
mada oso made no
asobi some

New Year's saké–
until the next,
this first delight

屠蘇酒や
又とそまでの
遊びそめ

kigo: toso (New Year's saké)

hatsu yume ya
samete mo hana wa
hana-gokoro

first dream—
even after awakening
the flower's heart the same

初
夢
や

さ
め
て
も
花
は

は
な
ご
こ
ろ

kigo: hatsu yume (first dream)

Note: In Japan there is a custom of attaching importance to the first things done in the New Year, like the first dream. The Japanese saying is *ichi Fuji, ni taka, san nasubi* (It is auspicious to dream first of Mount Fuji, second of a hawk, and third of an egglant).

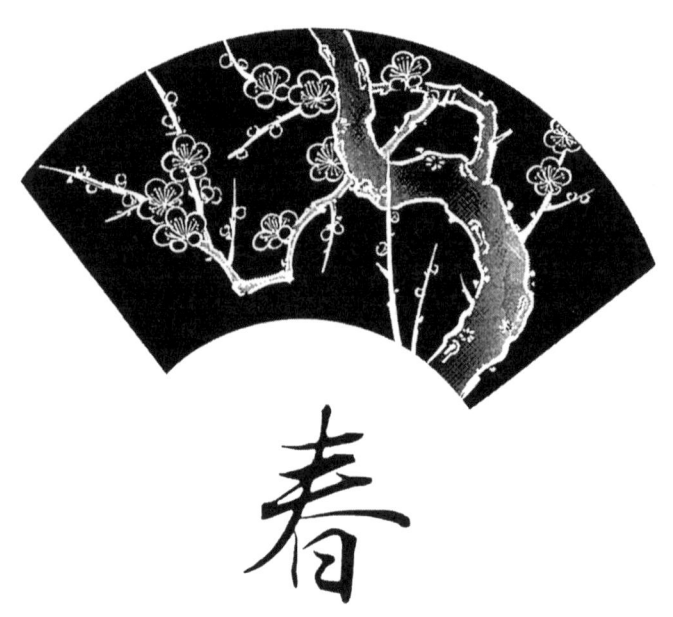

tsukikage mo
tatazumu ya hana no
asaborake

the moon's shadow
also pauses—
cherry-blossom dawn

月<ruby>影<rt>かげ</rt></ruby><ruby>月<rt>つき</rt></ruby>も
たたずむや<ruby>花<rt>はな</rt></ruby>の
あさぼらけ

kigo: hana (Although *hana* is generally defined as flower, in haiku it always refers to the cherry blossom.)

Note: Because the moon's shadow remains longer at dawn in the springtime, it seems to be also stopping in the sky to view the beautiful blossoms.

yo no hana wo
marū tsutsumu ya
oboro-zuki

wrapped around
this world's flower—
hazy moon

世_よの花_{はな}を
丸_{まる}うつゝむや
朧_{おぼろづき}月

kigo: oboro-zuki (hazy moon)

Note: To accentuate the feeling of the wrapping-around image, the repetition of the sounds *o* and *u* in Japanese adds to the warm, round feeling.

kagerō ya
hoshite wa nururu
ishi no ue

the shimmering haze
above
the wet stone

陽炎や
ほしてはぬるゝ
石の上

kigo: kagerō (shimmering haze)

Note: This haiku is included in the *Chiyo-ni no Issho* (Chiyo-ni's Life) poetry collection, but is not in the *Zenshu* (Collected Works).

wakakusa ya
kirema kirema ni
mizu no iro

green grass–
between, between the blades
the color of the water

若くさや
きれまきれまに
水のいろ

kigo: wakakusa (green grass)

ume ga ka ya
doko e fukaruru
yuki onna

plum flower scent–
where has the snow woman's
ghost blown to?

梅が香や
何所へ吹る〻
雪女

kigo: ume (plum flower)

Note: A *yuki onna* (snow woman) is a figure from Japanese folk legend. She is the ghost of a beautiful woman who only appears when it snows, and is both seductive and terrifying because her victims usually die after being seduced.

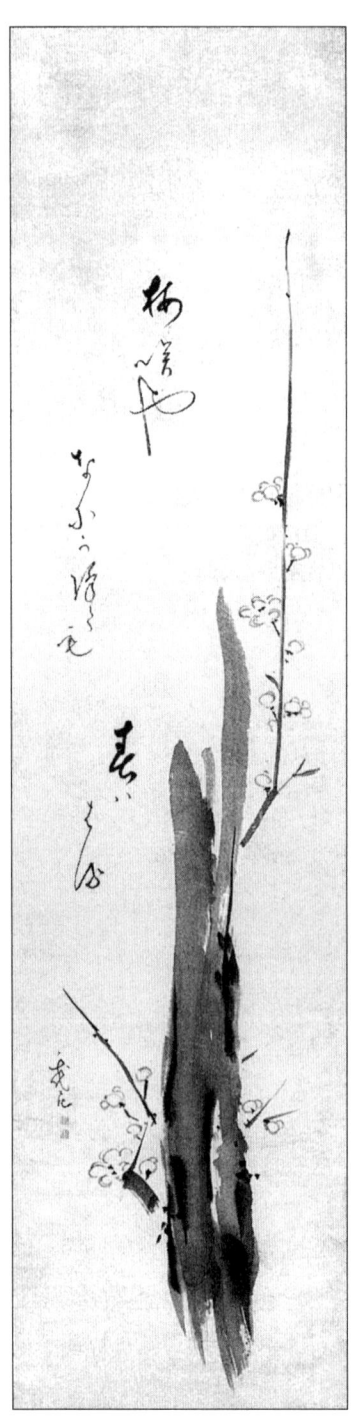

9. Chiyo-ni's *haiga* on her plum-blossom haiku: *ume saku ya / nani ga futte mo / haru wa haru* (flowering plum– / whether rain or snow falls / spring is spring). Matto City Museum.

compassion instead of revenge

taoraruru
hito ni kaoru ya
ume no hana

to the one breaking it–
the fragrance
of the plum

手折<ruby>た<rt></rt></ruby>らる<ruby>お<rt></rt></ruby>ゝ
人<ruby>ひと<rt></rt></ruby>に薫<ruby>かお<rt></rt></ruby>るや
梅<ruby>うめ<rt></rt></ruby>の花<ruby>はな<rt></rt></ruby>

kigo: ume (plum flower)

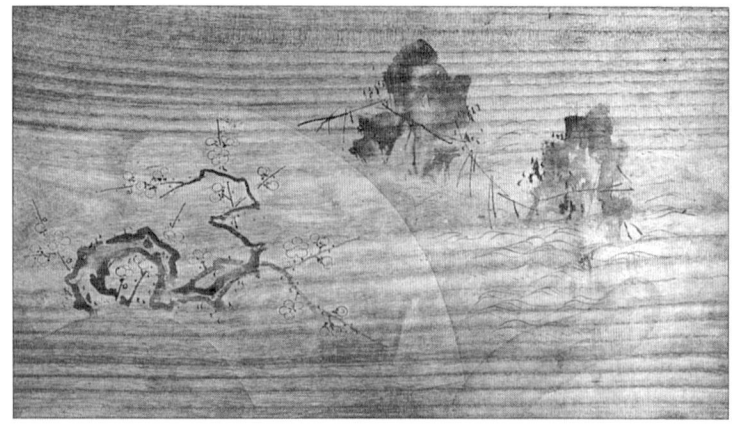

(TOP OF TABLE)

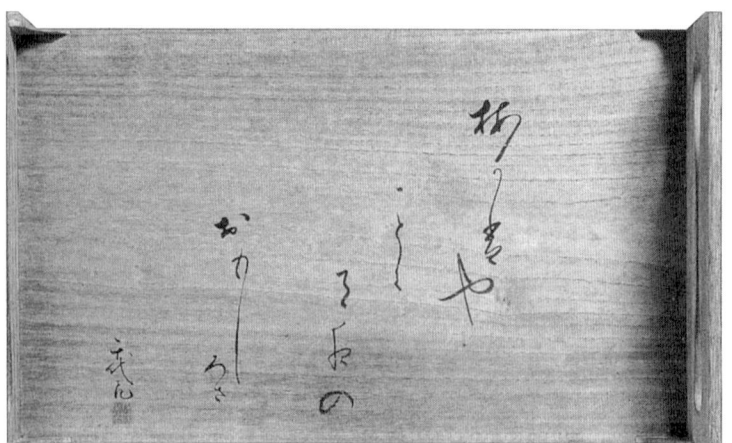

(UNDERSIDE)

10. Chiyo-ni's haiku and painting on a low table.
Above (top of table), a plum tree in blossom.
Below (underside), the haiku *ume ga ka ya / koto ni tsukiyo no / omoshirosa* (plum fragrance- / especially pleasing / on a moonlit night). Matto City Museum.

ume ga ka ni
shiroki meshi kū
yo nari keri

to be in a world
eating white rice
amid plum fragrance

梅が香に
白き飯くふ
世なりけり

kigo: ume (plum flower)

Note: Eating white rice refers to times of peace when there were no wars or rationing, such as the Edo period when Chiyo-ni lived. She utters this haiku with deep appreciation.

The plum flower was transplanted from China and was Japan's favorite flower until nationalism grew in the eighth century and the *sakura* (cherry blossom), which is native to Japan, took its place. Yet, Chiyo-ni wrote many haiku about the plum blossom (forty-seven plum versus ninety-eight *sakura* haiku).

zōriya no
kite kikoe keri
hatsu-zakura

the sandal maker
has come—
the first cherry blossoms

ざうり家の
来て聞えけり
初ざくら

kigo: hatsu-zakura (first cherry blossoms)

Note: As the spring comes, people in the colder, northern region anxiously wait for the flowers to bloom. Here the sandal maker brings news of the first cherry blossoms farther south.

The interest in *sakura* from ancient times was as much for its beauty as it was for its being a harbinger of spring and the harvest. It was thought that if the cherry blossoms fell quickly it forboded a bad rice crop in the autumn.

iriai o
sora ni osayuru
sakura kana

evening temple bell
stopped in the sky
by cherry blossoms

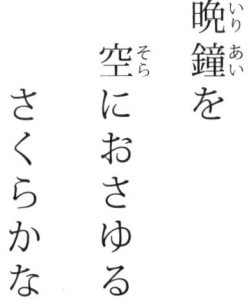

kigo: sakura (cherry blossoms)

Note: This haiku depicts the striking traditional beauty of *sakura* (cherry blossoms), to which a woman's beauty was often compared as in the court poetry of the Heian period (794–1186). Also, from a Buddhist perspective, this haiku depicts a moment of nonduality when the mind is stopped.

chōchō ya
nani o yume mite
hane tsukai

butterfly–
what's it dreaming
fanning its wings?

蝶々や
何を夢見て
羽つかひ

kigo: chōchō (butterfly)

Note: This is a reference to a classical Chinese story from Chuang Tzu, the Taoist philosopher (ca. 300 B.C.) who wondered if he were a man dreaming he was a butterfly or a butterfly dreaming he was a man.

chōchō ya
onago no michi no
ato ya saki

a butterfly
in front and back
of the woman's path

蝶々や
をなごの道の
跡や先

kigo: chōchō (butterfly)

Note: Traditionally, the butterfly in East Asia is often a symbol for women. Chiyo-ni frequently used this image to create a delicate, sensual feeling. *Michi* (path) could be literal as well as figurative, as a life path.

akebono no
wakare wa motanu
hi-i-na kana

dawn's separation
unknown
to dolls

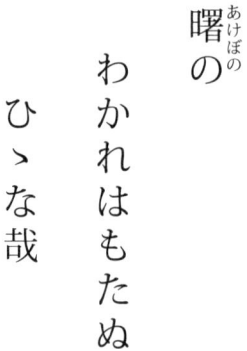

kigo: hina (dolls); *hi-i-na* for syllable count

Note: Written for Hinamatsuri or "The Doll's Festival," a traditional holiday for girls held on March third. Chiyo-ni uses the image of the doll to heighten the contrast of human sorrow in lovers' separation.

A similar haiku is said to embody the secret of Chiyo-ni's life, that before she became a nun she also knew the pains of love:

待暮も　曙もなき　紙衣かな
matsu kure mo / akebono mo naki / kamiko kana
no more waiting / for the evening or the dawn – / touching the old clothes

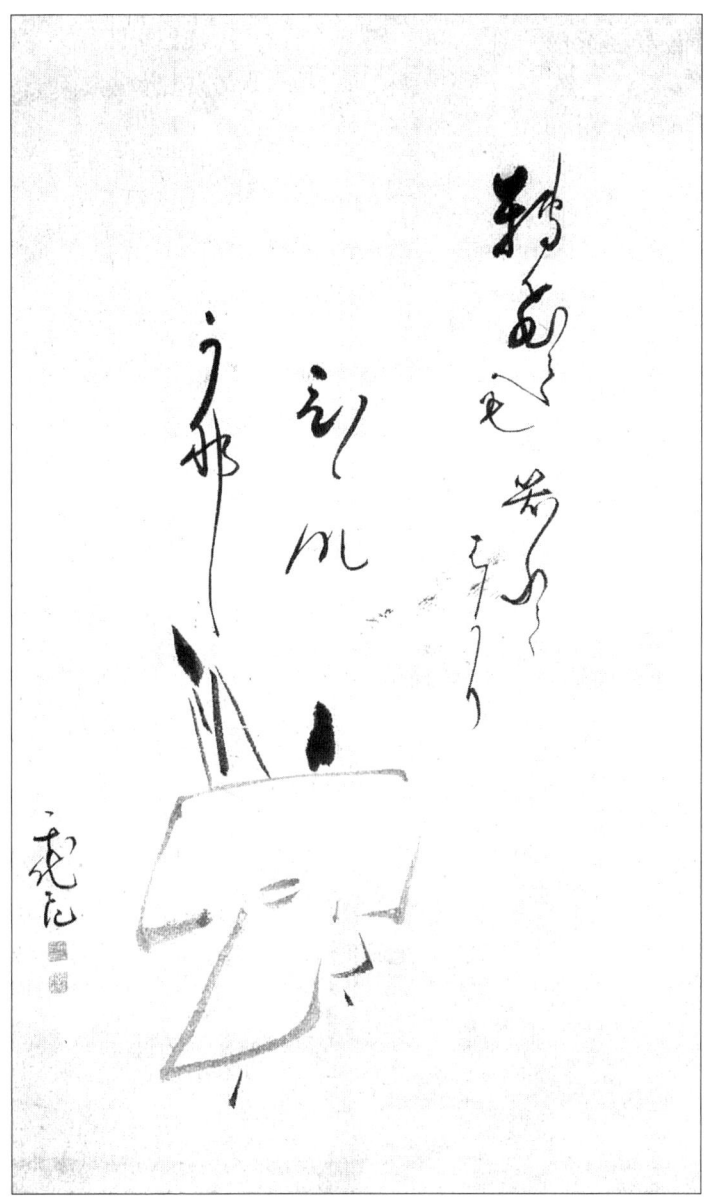

11. A *haiga* on the Hinamatsuri (Doll's Festival), with the haiku *korobite mo / warōte bakari / hi-i-na kana* (even falling down / it still smiles- / the festival doll), by Chiyo-ni at around age sixty-four. Matto City Museum.

asa yū ni
shizuku no futoru
konome kana

morning and evening
the dew swells
on the buds

朝夕_{あさゆう}に
雫_{しずく}のふとる
このめ哉_{かな}

kigo: konome (buds)

ne o tsukete
onago no yoku ya
sumire-sō

woman's desire
deeply rooted–
the wild violets

根_ねを付_{つけ}て
女子_{おなご}の欲_{よく}や
菫草_{すみれそう}

kigo: sumire (wild violets)

Note: An unusually powerful, direct, and sensual haiku for a woman of her time.

musubō to
tokō to kaze no
yanagi kana

to tangle or untangle
the willow—
it's up to the wind

結ふと
解ふと風の
やなぎかな

kigo: yanagi (willow)

Note: Chiyo-ni often used (in forty-one haiku) the image of the willow, whose delicate nature is traditionally a symbol for woman's beauty in East Asia.

koe tatenu
toki ka wakare zo
neko no koi

when not making a sound
is it their separation—
cats' love?

声<ruby>こえ</ruby>たてぬ
時<ruby>とき</ruby>かわかれぞ
猫<ruby>ねこ</ruby>の恋<ruby>こい</ruby>

kigo: neko no koi (cats' love)

chōchō no
tsumadatete iru
shiohi kana

the butterfly
is standing on tiptoes
at the ebb tide

蝶々^{ちょうちょう}の
つまたてゝ居^いる
しほ干^ひかな

kigo: shiohi (ebb tide) and *chōchō* (butterfly)

Note: In Chiyo-ni's time, sometimes two or more *kigo* (seasonal references) were used instead of one, as in this haiku. Later scholars categorized the haiku according to whichever *kigo* they felt was the strongest.

hirou mono
mina ugoku nari
shio higata

everything I pick up
is alive–
ebb tide

拾
ふ
も
の

み
な
動
く
な
り

塩
干
潟

kigo: shio higata (ebb tide)

103

tsukubōte
kumo o ukagau
kaeru kana

squatting
the frog observes
the clouds

踞_{つくぼ}ばふて
雲_{くも}を伺_{うかがう}ふ
蛙_{かえる}かな

kigo: kaeru (frog)

Note: This haiku echoes the work of the later poet Issa (1762–1826). He was also a Jodo-Shinshu Buddhist and wrote compassionately about tiny creatures. Another frog poem:

雨雲に　はらのふくるる　蛙かな
ama-gumo ni hara no fukururu kaeru kana
rain clouds– / the belly of the frog / puffs out!

kake izuru
koma mo ashi kagu
sumire kana

galloping horses also
smell their legs–
the wild violets

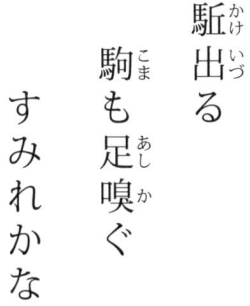

kigo: sumire (wild violets)

Note: As the horses trample the grassy field of wildflowers, the scent
of the violets clings to their legs.

omoi wasure
omoidasu hi zo
haru no shika

I forget
to remember the days—
yet these spring deer

思ひわすれ
思ひ出す日ぞ
春の鹿

kigo: haru no shika (spring deer)

Note: This was written in Chiyo-ni's later years. Because of the forgetfulness that comes with her old age, she feels in sharp contrast to the young deer; yet at the same time, she appreciates the moment.

tsukutsukushi
kokora ni tera no
ato mo ari

among a field
of horsetail weeds–
temple ruins

つくつくし
こゝらに寺_{てら}の
跡_{あと}もあり

kigo: tsukutsukushi (horsetail weeds)

oshinabete
koe naki chō mo
nori no niwa

even the butterfly
voiceless–
Buddhist service

をしなべて
声なき蝶も
法の場

kigo: chōchō (butterfly)

Note: This haiku was written for Shinran (the founder of Jodo-Shin-shu Buddhism) on the 500th anniversary of his death (Chiyo-ni was around sixty years old).

In another haiku, Chiyo-ni uses the butterfly to display something else entirely—the universality of moods and emotion, in this case, anger:

蝶々や　なれも腹たつ　日のあらむ
chōchō ya nare mo hara tatsu hi no aran
butterfly– / you also get mad / some days

kiji naite
tsuchi iro iro no
kusa to naru

the pheasant sings—
the earth turns into
various grasses

きじ啼て
土いろいろの
草となる

kigo: kiji (pheasant)

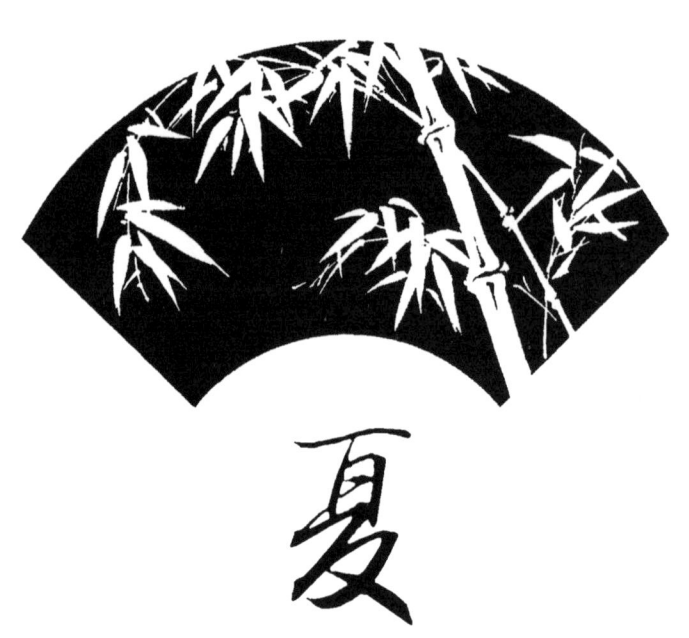

tsurizao no
ito ni sawaru ya
natsu no tsuki

touching
the fishing line–
the summer moon

釣
竿
の

糸
に
さ
は
る
や

夏
の
月

kigo: natsu no tsuki (summer moon)

mono no oto
mizu ni iru yo ya
hototogisu

sounds enter the water
on this night–
hototogisu

ものゝ音
水に入夜や
ほとゝぎす

kigo: hototogisu (cuckoo or nightingale)

Note: The cuckoo or nightingale, which is native to Japan, is called a *hototogisu*, a word which is onomatopoetic in Japanese. Its name sounds like the call of the bird.

tsuki suzushi
ano ha kono ha ni
tada okazu

the moon's coolness—
on that leaf, this leaf
not only light

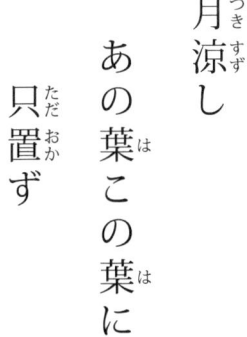

kigo: tsuki suzushi (moon's coolness)

suzushisa ya
yo fukaki hashi ni
shiranu dōshi

keeping cool–
in the deep night
strangers on the bridge

涼しさや
夜ふかき橋に
しらぬ同士

kigo: suzushisa (coolness)

suzushisa ya
suso karamo fuku
yabu tatami

the coolness—
of the bottom of her kimono
in the bamboo grove

涼<ruby>す<rt></rt></ruby>しさや
裾<ruby>す<rt></rt></ruby>からも吹<ruby>ふ<rt></rt></ruby>く
薮<ruby>や<rt></rt></ruby>たゝみ

kigo: suzushisa (coolness)

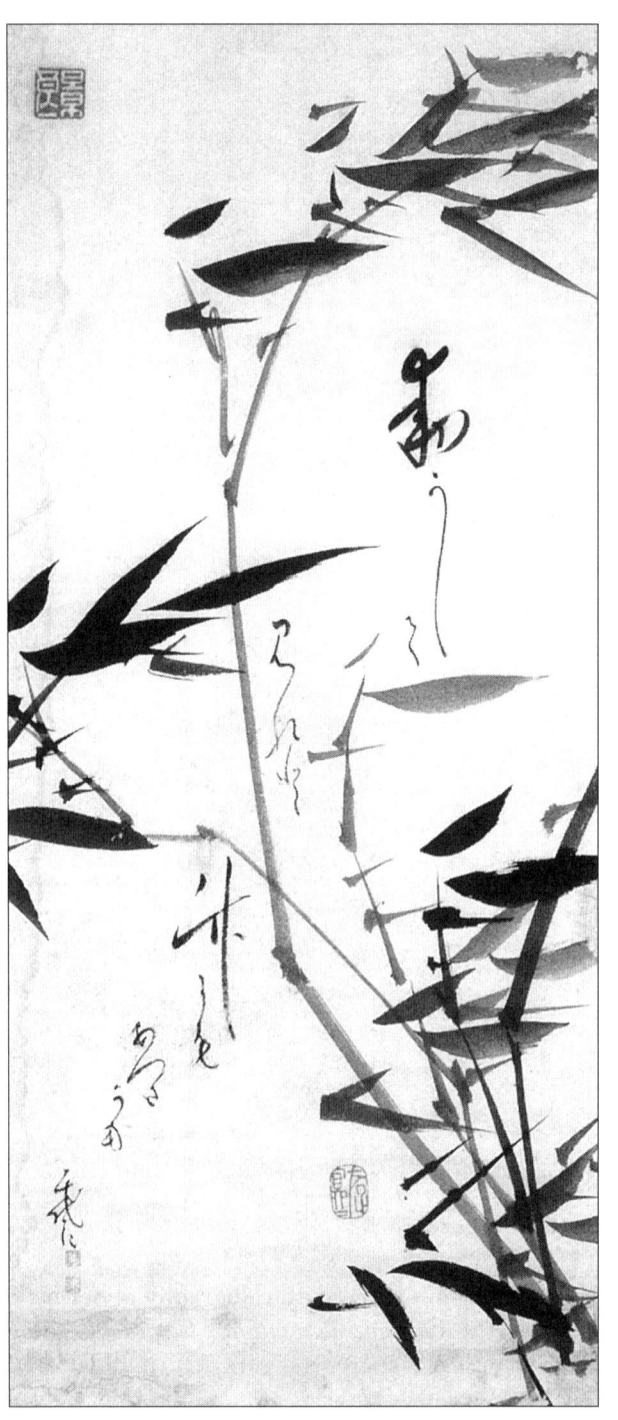

12. One of a set of three scrolls done in Chiyo-ni's later years: a *haiga* with Chi-yo-ni's calligraphy of her haiku about the bamboo, *ugokashite / miredo take ni mo / at-susa kana* (shaking the bamboo – / yet even it / has its own heat). Illustrated by Ryotai. Matto City Museum.

suzukaze ya
tamoto ni shimete
ne-iru made

cool breeze–
enclosed in my kimono sleeves
till falling asleep

涼風や
袂にしめて
寝入るまで

kigo: suzukaze (cool breeze)

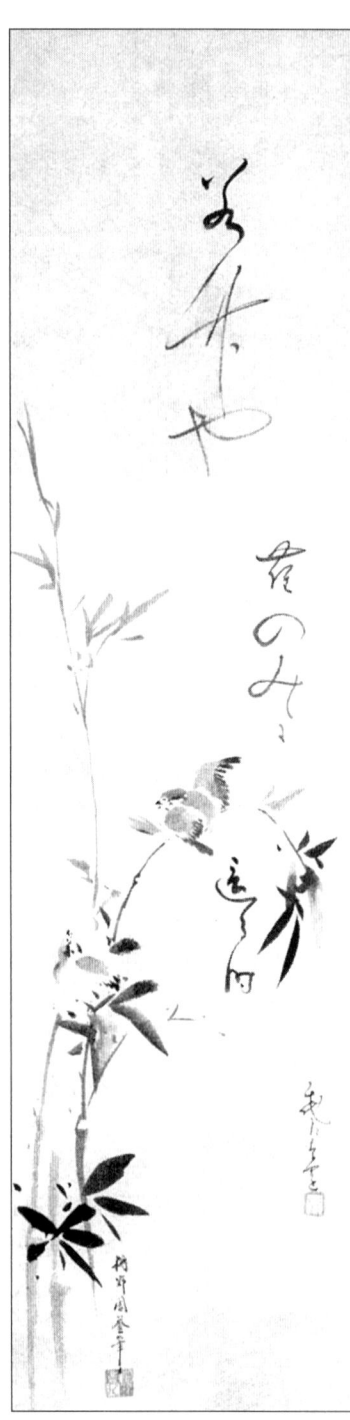

13. Chiyo-ni's *haiga* with calligraphy of her haiku on young bamboo: *waka-take ya / suzume no mimi ni / hairu toki* (sound of young bamboo / when it enters / sparrows' ears …). Illustrated by Shuyo Kano. Matto City Museum.

hana no ka ni
ushiro misete ya
koromogae

change of kimono:
showing only her back
to the blossom's fragrance

花
の
香
に
うしろ見せてや
更衣

kigo: koromogae (seasonal change of kimono)

Note: Koromogae is the name for the seasonal ritual of changing one's kimono, here from winter to summer. This haiku exemplifies Chiyo-ni's extremely subtle and sensual imagery.

kaketaranu
onna-gokoro ya
doyōboshi

airing out kimonos
as well as her heart
is never enough

かけたらぬ
女心や
土用干

kigo: doyōboshi (airing out)

Note: The custom of "airing out" is done in summer to prevent kimonos, books, scrolls, and so on from being eaten by insects and mold. Here, there is also a subtext of frustration, probably stemming from the suppression of women in Edo society.

yūgao ya
mono no kakurete
utsukushiki

moonflowers–
the beauty
of hidden things

ゆ ふ が ほ や
物 の の か く れ て
う つ く し き

kigo: yūgao (moonflowers)

Note: The moonflower blooms in the dusk, unfolding its whiteness faintly at first and then more so as the night darkens.

yūgao ya
onago no hada no
miyuru toki

moonflowers!
when a woman's skin
is revealed

夕顔や
女子の肌の
見ゆる時

kigo: yūgao (moonflowers)

Note: This white flower, which only blooms in the evening, heightens the sensuality of skin in the dark; it is also a reference to a lover of the prince in *The Tale of Genji*. Here is a related haiku:

行くすえは　誰が肌ふれん　紅の花
yuku-sue wa ta ga hada furen beni no hana
eventually / whose skin will they touch– / the rouge flower?

Rouge makeup was traditionally made from the safflower or rouge flower; this haiku was originally attributed to Basho, but it is now believed by a few to be one of Chiyo-ni's—"Some say it is Chiyo-ni's haiku—probably so, not Basho's tone," said Kan-in in the book *Basho Hokku-shu Setsu*, 1798.

beni saita
kuchi mo wasururu
shimizu kana

rouged lips
forgotten–
clear springwater

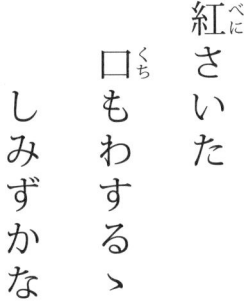

kigo: shimizu (clear springwater)

Note: This is one of Chiyo-ni's best and most memorable realization haiku; she wrote four versions of this haiku at different stages of her life, showing not only her dedication as an artist, but her progression of realization as well. This last one, written at age sixty-two, shows her forgetting her rouged lips (the makeup which was so important to women of her time) while drinking the fresh water. This haiku expresses the heightened awareness that comes when one forgets the self and the mind is present to the moment.

michi no ki no
fude nimo musubu
shimizu kana

she also cups
the springwater
for her travel writing brush

道の記の
筆にも結ぶ
清水かな

kigo: shimizu (springwater)

Note: When traveling in the Edo period, poets usually carried an ink-and-brush box to write with. This haiku shows Chiyo-ni's devotion to her art—writing spontaneously on the road—and may also show her affinity toward her writing brush.

koborete wa
moto no mizu nari
beni no tsuyu

when dropped
it is only water–
rouge flower dew

こぼれては
もとの水なり
紅の露

kigo: beni no hana (rouge flower, safflower)

Note: Another variant of this haiku uses the word *tada* (only) instead of *moto* (originally) in Japanese. This haiku epitomizes Chiyo-ni's ability to see things as they are as well as her clear writing style. In it, she uses one of her most frequently used images, water (in 35 haiku).

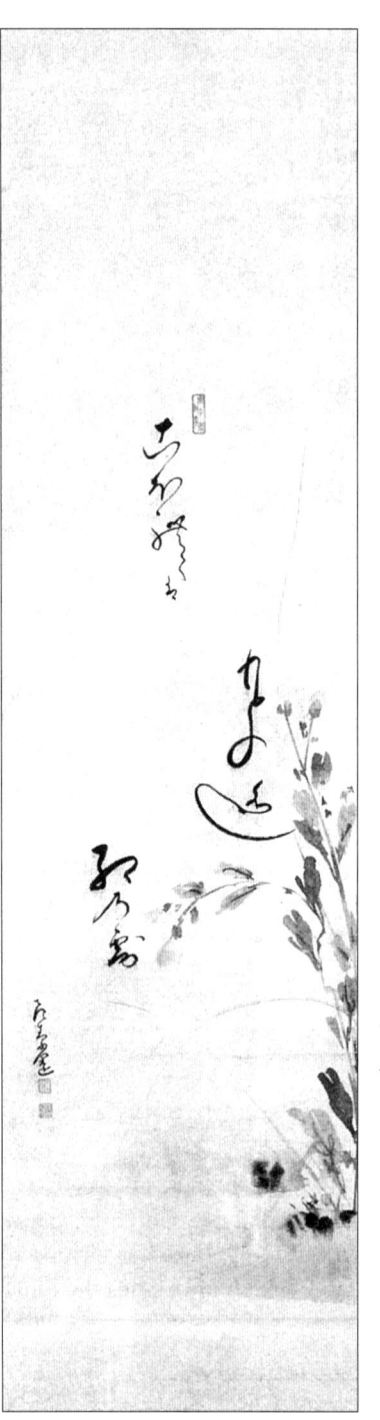

14. A *haiga* with Chiyo-ni's calligraphy of her rouge-flower haiku. Illustrated by Shijoken Yada. Matto City Museum.

hototogisu
mada shirakami no
aware nari

cuckoo–
still a blank paper
how lonely

杜
鵑
まだ白紙の
あはれなり

kigo: hototogisu (cuckoo)

Note: In this haiku, we can imagine Chiyo-ni, paper and brush in hand, waiting for the cuckoo's cry to inspire her writing. As she waits, without a cry, she is disappointed, which intensifies the loneliness of the night.

taki no ne mo
hosoru ya mine ni
semi no koe

sound of the waterfall
diminishes in the peaks–
cicadas' voices

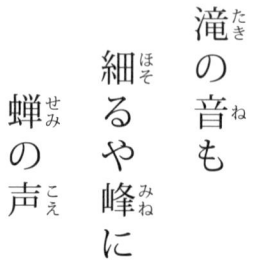

kigo: semi (cicada)

Note: Another cicada haiku:

はつ蝉は　どの木ともなし　聞ばかり
hatsu semi wa dono ki to mo nashi kiku bakari
first cicada– / hearing only this / from an unknown tree

mada kami no
musubanu mo idete
taue kana

again the women
come to the fields
with unkempt hair

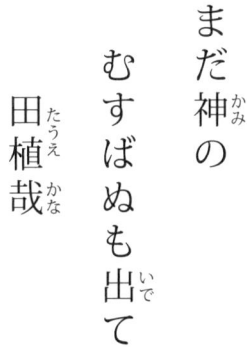

kigo: taue (rice planting)

Note: This haiku depicts women too busy in the ricefields every day to worry about the beauty of their hair. Chiyo-ni was using word-play with the word *kami* which can be read as "hair" (as in the above translation) or as "god/goddess." Here is a related haiku:

けふばかり　男をつかふ　田植えかな
kyō bakari otoko o tsukau taue kana
just for today / using men / for rice-planting

In the Edo period, most of the rice-planting was done by women, yet sometimes men were asked to help, so the word *tsukau* meaning *to use* could just be taken matter-of-factly; on the other hand, the tone of this word could also be seen as bold, unrefined or even feminist.

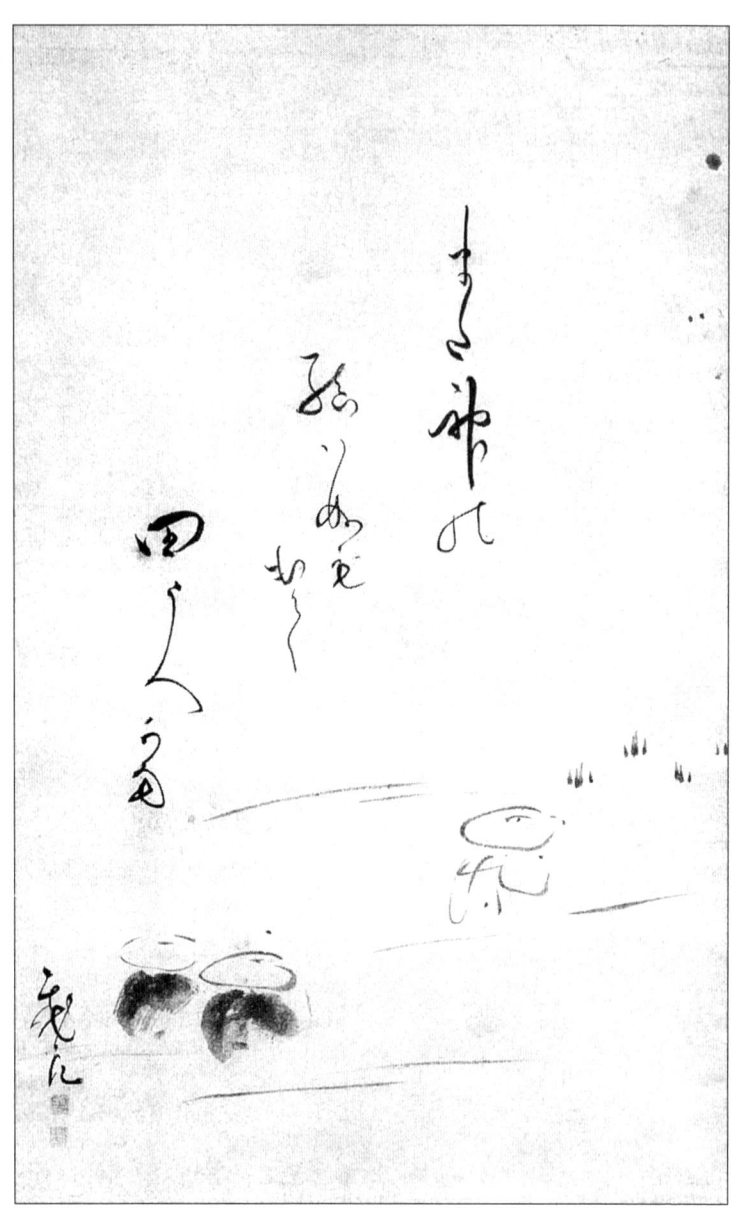

15. Chiyo-ni's *haiga* on women in the rice fields. Matto City Museum.

kayatsuri no
kusa mo sagete ya
hanamidō

mosquito-net grass
also hangs
at the flower shrine

蚊帳つりの
草もさげてや
花御堂

kigo: hanamidō (flower shrine)

Note: The flower shrine is used for the Hanamatsuri (Flower Festival) to commemorate Buddha's birthday on April eighth. Cherry blossoms and other seasonal flowers are usually used rather than mosquito-net grass, a common weed, to adorn the roof of the enshrined Buddha statue. Another haiku of humility:

ひとすじに　百合はうつむく　ばかり也
hitosuji ni yuri wa utsumuku bakari nari
the one true path / for the lily / is just to bow her head

tabako-ire
harōte modoru
suzumi kana

the coolness
emptying a tobacco box–
the return home

煙草入
<ruby>煙<rt>たぼ</rt></ruby><ruby>草<rt>こ</rt></ruby><ruby>入<rt>いれ</rt></ruby>
<ruby>払<rt>はろ</rt></ruby>ふて<ruby>戻<rt>もど</rt></ruby>る
すゞみかな

kigo: suzumi (coolness)

Note: Another coolness haiku:

松の葉も　よみつくすほど　涼けり
matsu no ha mo yomitsukusu hodo suzumi keri
counting pine needles / until / I become cool

kawa bakari
yami wa nagarete
hotaru kana

only in the river
darkness flows:
fireflies

川<ruby>かわ<rt>かわ</rt></ruby>ばかり
闇<ruby>やみ<rt>やみ</rt></ruby>はながれて
蛍<ruby>ほたる<rt>ほたる</rt></ruby>かな

kigo: hotaru (fireflies)

Note: Fireflies were prevalent and cherished in Chiyo-ni's time; another firefly haiku:

しのゝめや　とめし蛍を　置忘れ
shinonome ya tomeshi hotaru o okiwasure
clouds at dawn– / yesterday's / fireflies forgotten

For a woman's death

kumo no yukari
soreka to bakari
kakitsubata

purple cloud—
isn't it the same color
as the iris?

雲
の
ゆ
か
り
そ
れ
か
と
ば
か
り
杜
若

kigo: kakitsubata (iris)

Note: This is said to be a mourning haiku for Chiyo-ni's mother. The purple cloud represents cremation smoke. Also, in some sects of Buddhism it is said that if a dying person chants the name of Buddha, he will descend on a purple cloud to take the person to an enlightened state or paradise.

Truth is one

shimizu ni wa
ura mo omote mo
nakari keri

clear water:
no front
no back

清水には
裏も表も
なかりけり

kigo: shimizu (clear water)

Note: This haiku reflects Chiyo-ni's Buddhist perspective on the coemergence of all phenomena as one—the good, the bad, the happy, and the sad.

shimizu suzushi
hotaru no kiete
nani mo nashi

clear water is cool
fireflies vanish–
there's nothing more

清水すゞし
蛍のきえて
なにもなし

kigo: hotaru (fireflies)

Note: This is one of her two *jisei*, or death poems, the last haiku she wrote in her own hand a few weeks before she died in 1775. Chiyo-ni often used the firefly image (in nineteen haiku) to represent the ephemeral. There are four versions of this haiku, which shows her dedication as a writer despite being physically weak, as well as her clear and detached state of mind, even as death approached.

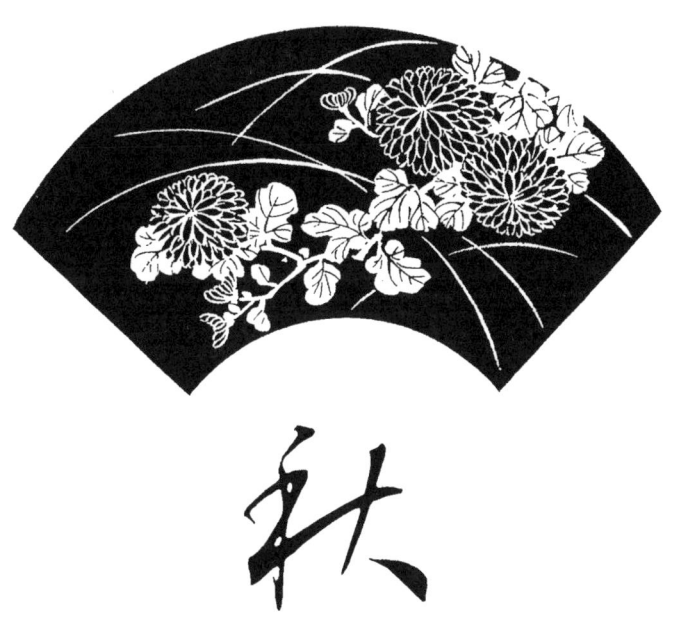

mikazuki ni
hishihishi to mono no
shizumarinu

at the crescent moon
the silence
enters the heart

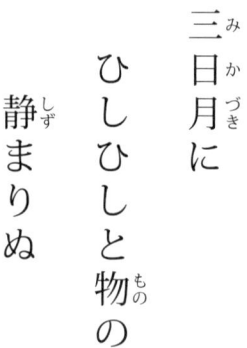

kigo: mikazuki (crescent moon)

Note: The word *hishihishi* is almost untranslatable, but implies an emotion or awareness that enters one's being deeply, little by little. In this case, loneliness.

When invited here for the first time

> *yūgure o*
> *yoso ni azukete*
> *momiji kana*

> twilight
> is left
> in the maple leaves

ゆ
ふ
ぐ
れ
を

余
所（よ・そ）
に
預（あず）
け
て

も
み
ぢ
哉（かな）

kigo: momiji (maple leaves)

Note: In the autumn of 1760 when Chiyo-ni was fifty-eight, she went to Zuisenji temple in Etchu to attend the 500th memorial service for Shinran (1173–1262), the founder of Jodo-Shinshu Buddhism. She was honored to stay at Honjin Inn, an exclusive inn for *daimyo*, great landowners. It was in that beautiful garden that she wrote this haiku.

139

meigetsu ya
me ni okinagara
tōaruki

full moon–
keeping it in my eyes
on a distant walk

名月_{めいげつ}や
眼_めに置_{おき}ながら
遠_{とう}歩_{ある}行_き

kigo: meigetsu (full moon)

Note: In this poem, the moon is a symbol of realization. Chiyo-ni is walking on the spiritual path in the light of the moon, which symbolizes compassion and the cooling of desire.

meigetsu ni
kaerite hanasu
koto wa nashi

moon viewing–
after coming home
nothing to say

名月に
帰て咄す
事はなし

kigo: meigetsu (full moon)

Note: This haiku is a humble admission that even a poet is sometimes at a loss for words.

hatsukari ya
iyoiyo nagaki
yo ni kawari

first wild geese–
the nights are becoming long,
becoming long

初雁や
いよいよながき
夜にかはり

kigo: hatsukari (first wild geese)

Note: Wild geese appear in Japan in early autumn and signal that the autumn nights are getting longer.

Another haiku echoing long nights:

長き夜や　かはりがはりに　虫の声
nagaki yo ya kawari-gawari ni mushi no koe
the long night– / turn by turn / insects' voices

tsuki no yo ya
ishi ni dete naku
kirigirisu

moonlit night–
a cricket sings
out on a stone

月の夜や
石に出て啼
きりぎりす

kigo: kirigirisu (cricket)

Note: Another haiku which shows Chiyo-ni's identification with small creatures. The *matsutake* mushroom is found under the pine tree, so the mushroom may be like an umbrella to little insects:

まつ茸や　あれもなにかの　雨やどり
matsutake ya are mo nanika no amayadori
matsutake– / but also / a rain shelter

143

izayoi no
yami o kobosu ya
imo no tsuyu

sixteenth night–
darkness drops
in the dew on taro leaves

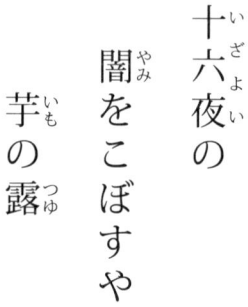

kigo: izayoi (sixteenth night)

Note: Izayoi refers to either the night or the moon of August sixteenth, the day after the full moon, so it implies a hesitant moon having another kind of subtler beauty. Also, in Japanese a kind of wordplay is used—the verb *kobosu* (drops) modifies both the *yami* (darkness) and *tsuyu* (dew); this beautiful delicate image is of the night darkening and this darkness being reflected in the dewdrops, little by little. This poetic device is similar to the one on page 169.

Another related haiku:

十六夜や　まだ誰だれも　見えぬうち
izayoi ya mada dare dare mo mienu uchi
sixteenth night moon– / before anyone / anyone comes

144

uramachi no
ibiki akarushi
kyō no tsuki

back streets' snoring
and today's full moon
(both) bright

うら町の
鼾あかるし
けふの月

kigo: tsuki (full moon)

Note: Here the word *akarushi* (bright), acts as a *kakekotoba* or pivot word, a Japanese poetic device which modifies both what comes before it (*ibiki* "snoring") and what comes after it (*tsuki* "full moon"), adding another level to the poem. This device also humorously shows the poet's nondualistic view that the world of heaven and the world of everyday life both share the bright light.

kaya no te o
hitotsu hazushite
tsukimi kana

the mosquito net
with a corner untied—
ah, the moon

蚕帳か の手て を
ひとつはずして
月見つきみ かな

kigo: double *kigo* of *kaya* (mosquito net) for summer and *tsukimi* (moonviewing) for autumn

Note: In Lafcadio Hearn's book, *In Ghostly Japan* (1899) containing one of the earliest translations of Chiyo-ni, he tells the story of how she wrote this haiku: "Chiyo-ni, having been challenged to make a poem of seventeen syllables referring to a square, a triangle, and a circle, she is said to have immediately responded with this haiku. The top of the net, represents the square, letting down the net at one corner converts the square into a triangle, and the moon represents the circle."

This popularly translated haiku is said to be Chiyo-ni's, but is not found in her canon.

mi-agari ni
hitori nezame no
yosamu kana

on her day off
the prostitute wakes up alone–
the night's chill

身あがりに
独ねざめの
夜寒哉

kigo: yosamu (night's chill)

Note: This expresses the feeling of *mono no aware* (poignancy) of a prostitute's double loneliness, that she even has to pay for her day off, when she is alone.

nuimono ni
hari no koboruru
uzura kana

at her sewing
the needle drops–
the quails' cry

縫_{ぬい}物_{もの}に
針_{はり}のこぼるゝ
鶉_{うずら}かな

kigo: uzura (quail)

Note: Another poignant haiku about quails:
売られても　秋をわすれぬ　鶉哉
uraretemo aki o wasurenu uzura kana
even when sold / the quail doesn't forget / the autumn

hoshiai ya
dochira kara mono
i-i somen

stars' meeting
which one
speaks first?

星合や
どちらから物
言そめん

kigo: hoshiai (stars' meeting)

Note: The Japanese Tanabata festival celebrates the myth of the Milky Way's star-crossed lovers, Altair and Vega. A related haiku is:

夕顔も　寝るやくそくぞ　ほしまつり
yūgao mo neru yakusoku zo hoshi matsuri
moonflowers, too / promise to sleep together– / star festival

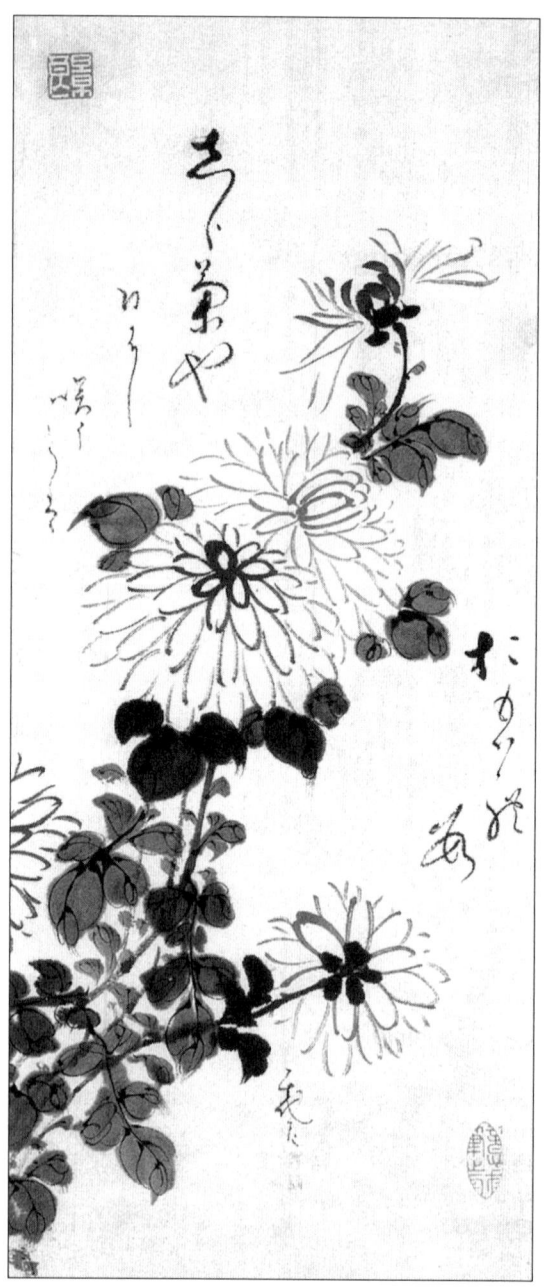

16. One of a set of three scrolls: a *haiga* with Chiyo-ni's calligraphy of her chrysanthemum haiku, *shiragiku ya / hi ni sakōto wa / omowarezu* (white chrysanthemum– / I didn't think / it would bloom in the sun). Illustrated by Ryotai. Matto City Museum.

shiragiku ya
beni saita te no
osoroshiki

how terrifying
her rouged fingers
against the white chrysanthemum

白菊<ruby>白<rt>しら</rt></ruby><ruby>菊<rt>ぎく</rt></ruby>や
<ruby>紅<rt>べに</rt></ruby>さいた<ruby>手<rt>て</rt></ruby>の
おそろしき

kigo: shiragiku (white chrysanthemum)

asagao ya
tsurube torarete
morai mizu

morning glory–
the well-bucket entangled
I ask for water

朝顔や
釣瓶とられて
もらひ水

kigo: asagao (morning glory)

Note: This is Chiyo-ni's most famous haiku. There are two versions—one using *asagao ya* and one using *asagao ni*; although the *ni* version appears in this *haiga* painting, we prefer the *ya* version since it heightens the emotion of the ah! moment as explained on p. 55, "The Haiku Form."

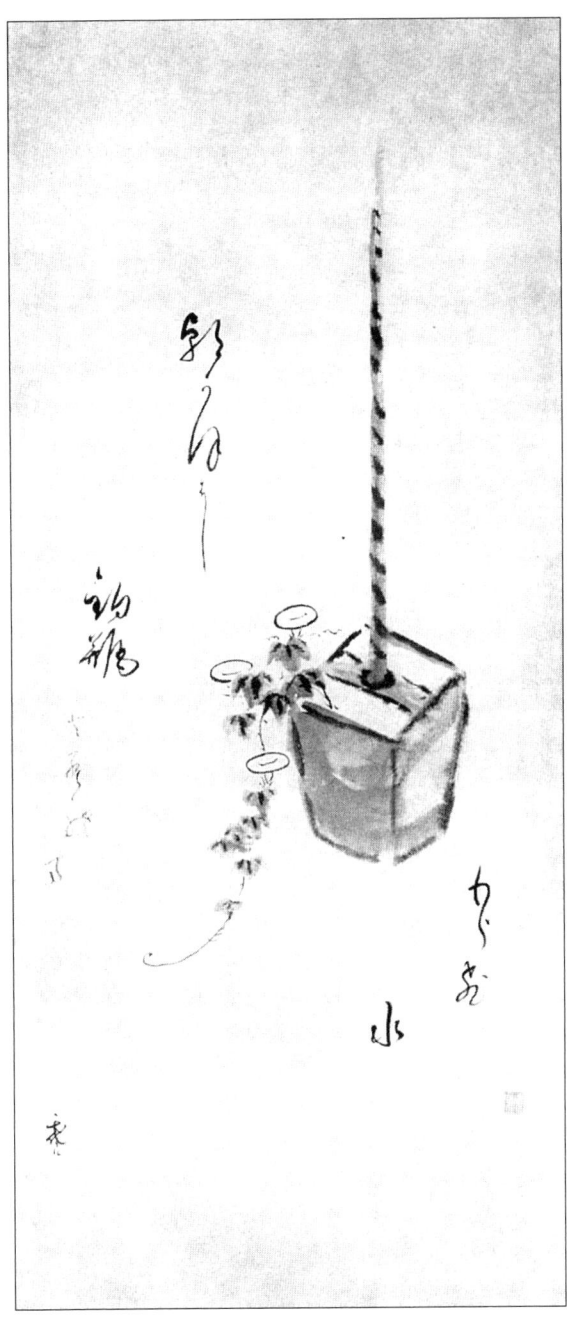

17. Left panel of a screen: a *haiga* with Chiyo-ni's calligraphy of her famous morning-glory haiku. Illustrated by Toho Naito. Matto City Museum.

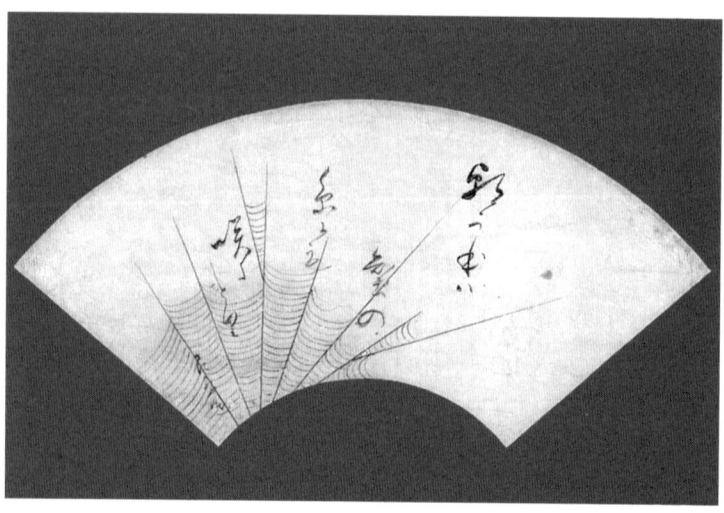

18. Chiyo-ni's *haiga* on fan-shaped paper inscribed with her haiku *asagao wa / kumo no ito ni mo / saki ni keri* (the morning glory– / has even bloomed / in the spiderweb). Matto City Museum.

asagao ya
makoto wa hana no
hito kirai

morning glory–
the truth is
the flower hates people

あさがほや

誠は花の

人きらひ

kigo: asagao (morning glory)

Note: Chiyo-ni wrote twenty-eight *asagao* or morning-glory haiku. The above haiku may be a reflection of her sense of humor about it all.

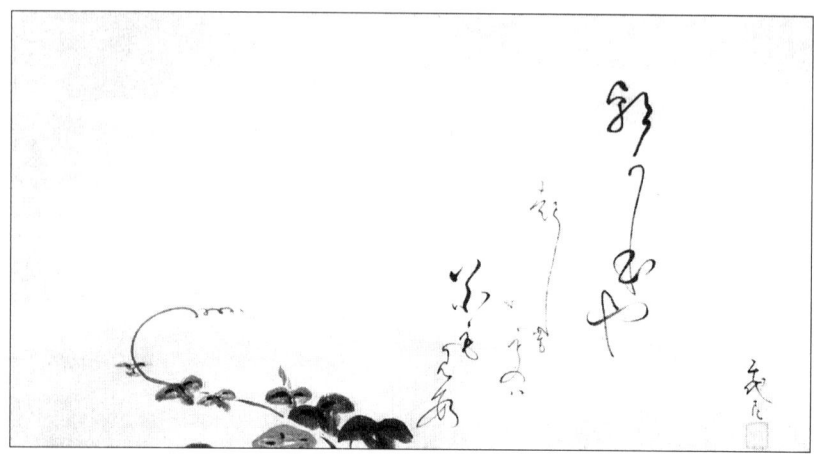

19. Chiyo-ni's *haiga* with her haiku *asagao ya / okoshita mono wa / hana mo mizu* (morning glory! / the one who raised it / didn't even notice it), done at age sixty. Matto City Museum.

yuku mizu ni
onoga kage ou
tonbo kana

over the flowing water
chasing its shadow–
the dragonfly

行^{ゆく}水^{みず}に
をのが影^{かげ}追^{おう}ふ
蜻^{とんぼ}蛉^{かな}哉

kigo: tonbo (dragonfly)

Note: This is another one of Chiyo-ni's well-known dragonfly haiku depicting the everyday world of women:

干物の　竿をせばめて　蜻蛉哉
hoshimono no sao o sebamete tonbo kana
the laundry pole / has become shorter– / dragonflies

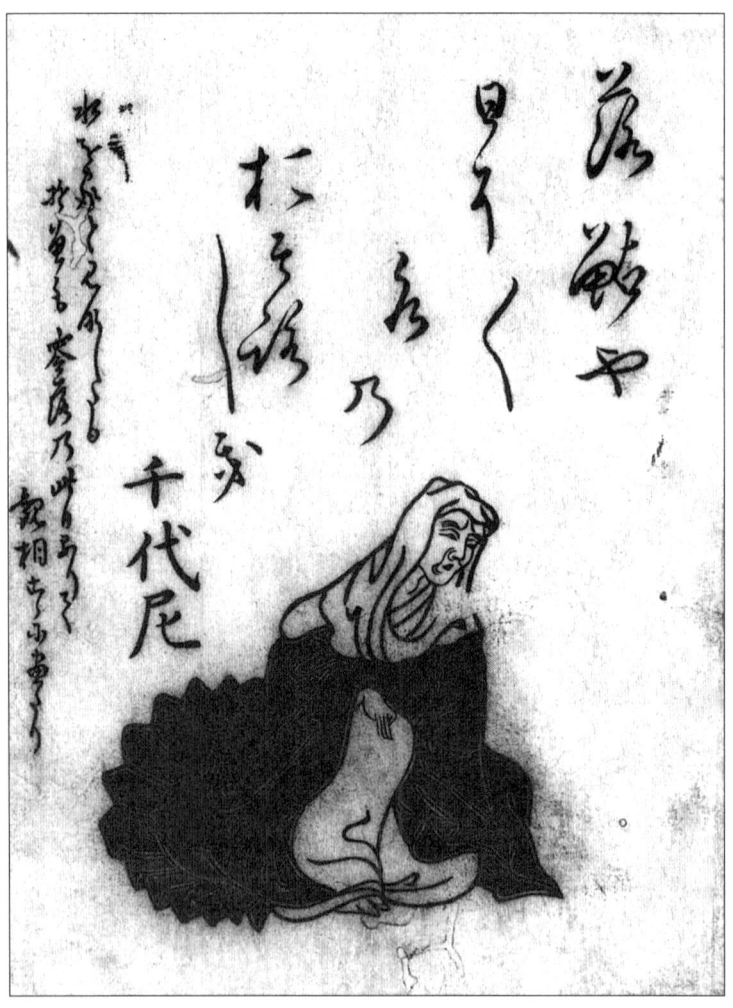

20. A woodblock portrait of Chiyo-ni with her haiku (ca. 1765), from *Haikai Hyakui-chi-Shu* (the One Hundred and One Poets collection), edited and illustrated by Koko Ozaki. Tokyo City Central Library.

ochiayu ya
hini hini mizu no
osoroshiki

dying sweetfish–
day by day
the water harsher

落鮎や
日に日に水の
おそろしき

kigo: ochiayu (dying sweetfish)

Note: In the autumn, sweetfish die after giving birth; this haiku shows both the harshness of the water as the weather gets colder, and her compassion for the fish. This haiku was included along with her portrait in the *Haikai Hyakuichi-Shu* (One Hundred and One Haiku Poets) in 1765.

akikaze no
yama o mawaru ya
kane no koe

the autumn wind
resounds in the mountain–
voice of the bell

秋風の
山をまはるや
鐘の声

kigo: akikaze (autumn wind)

oto sōte
ame ni shizumaru
kinuta kana

sounds merge–
the rain quiets
the pounding of cloth

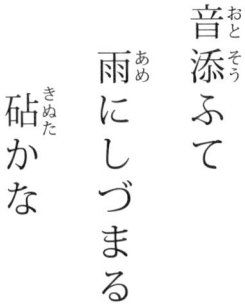

kigo: kinuta (a cloth pounder)

Note: The *kinuta* is a wooden hammer used to pound straw or cotton cloth, to make it softer and lustrous. In this haiku, the sound of the *kinuta* diminishes with the sound of the rain.

sangai yuishin (the Three Realms are one mind):

hyakunari ya
tsuru hitosuji no
kokoro yori

a hundred gourds
from the heart
of one vine

百生や
つる一すじの
心より

kigo: hyakunari (a hundred gourds)

Note: This haiku and the morning-glory haiku are Chiyo-ni's best-known works. When Chiyo-ni was twenty-four years old, a Zen master at Eiheiji temple asked her to write on the Buddhist theme *sankai* (the Three Realms): desire, form, and nonform. Much to his surprise, she answered with this haiku, showing her deep understanding that everything arises from the mind.

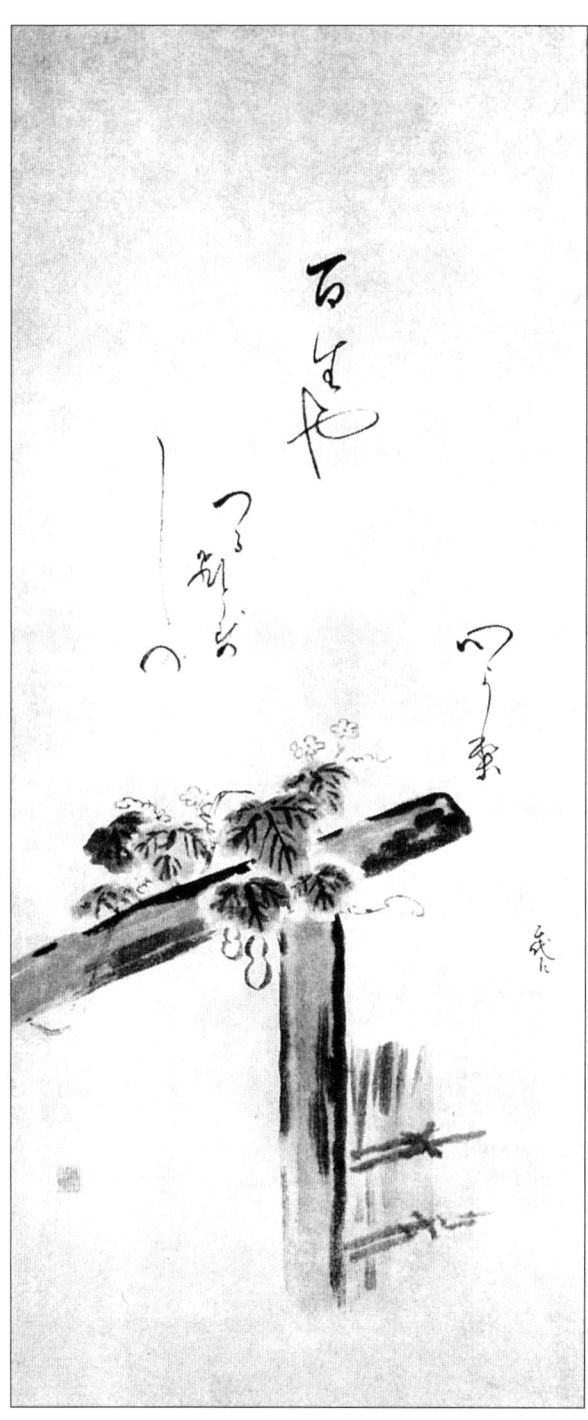

21. Right panel of a screen: *haiga* with Chiyo-ni's calligraphy of her famous gourd haiku. Illustrated by Toho Naito. Matto City Museum.

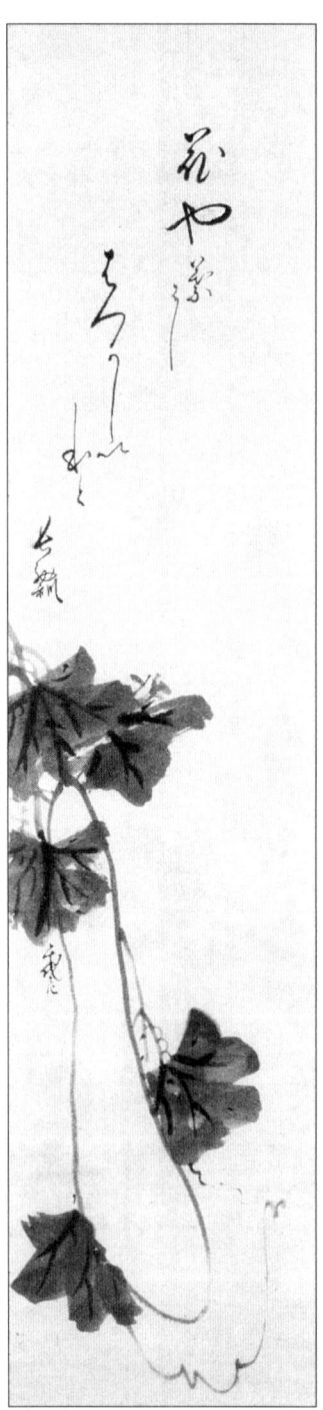

22. A *haiga* by Chiyo-ni at around age sixty-five with another one of her gourd haiku: *hana ya ha ni / hazukashii hodo / nagafukube* (its flowers and leaves / are ashamed– / the extra long gourd). Matto City Museum.

aki no no ya
hana to naru kusa
naranu kusa

autumn field–
some grasses flower
some grasses don't

秋<small>あき</small>の野<small>の</small>や
花<small>はな</small>となる草<small>くさ</small>
成<small>な</small>らぬ草<small>くさ</small>

kigo: aki no no (autumn field)

Note: This haiku articulates Chiyo-ni's acceptance of things as they are.

yume samenu
tatami ni kiku no
sakishi kyō

unfinished dream—
a chrysanthemum blooms
in the tatami room

夢^{ゆめ}さめぬ
畳^{たたみ}に菊^{きく}の
咲^{さき}しけふ

kigo: kiku (chrysanthemum)

Note: There is a story that while Chiyo-ni slept, someone put a flower by her pillow and when she awoke from a dream and was startled to see the flower, she felt incomplete in her dreamlike world, but then her heart became calm.

chō wa yume no
nagori wake iru
hana-no kana

traces of a dream—
a butterfly
through the flower field

蝶は夢の
名残わけ入る
花野哉

kigo: hanano (flower field)

Note: This haiku is a good example of both delicate female imagery and the feeling of *mujō*, the transiency of life.

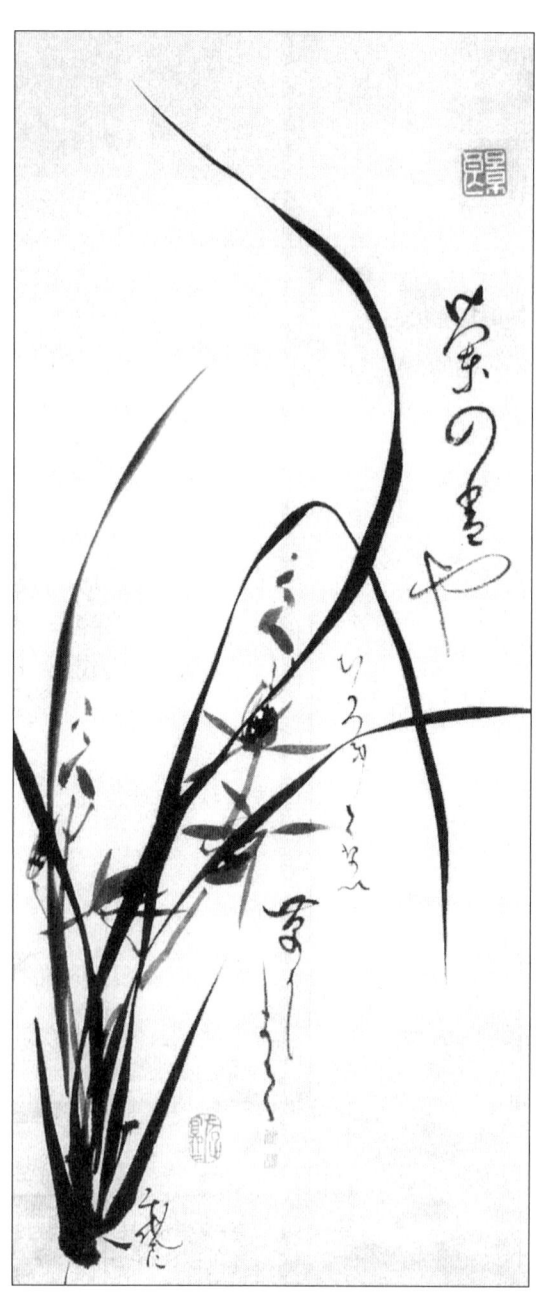

23. One of a set of
three scrolls: a *haiga*
with Chiyo-ni's
calligraphy of her
orchid haiku. Illus-
trated by Ryotai.
Matto City Museum.

ran no kaya
chikazuki denai
kusa ni made

fragrance of the orchid–
even to the grass
far away

蘭<ruby>ら<rt></rt></ruby>の香<ruby>か<rt></rt></ruby>や
ちかづきでない
草<ruby>くさ<rt></rt></ruby>にまで

kigo: ran (orchid)

tsuki mo mite
ware wa kono yo o
kashiku kana

I also saw the moon
and so I say goodbye
to this world

月<ruby>も見<rt>つき　み</rt></ruby>て
我<ruby>は<rt>われ</rt></ruby>この世<ruby>を<rt>よ</rt></ruby>
かしく哉<ruby><rt>かな</rt></ruby>

kigo: tsuki (moon)

Note: This is Chiyo-ni's last haiku, dictated to someone before her death. The "also" infers that she had experienced everything in life including the full autumn moon right before she died. The word *kashiku* was usually used by women in those days at the end of a letter to say goodbye; it shows her clear and calm state of mind.

Koko, a poet friend, wrote a mourning haiku for Chiyo-ni. Here, the "moon and flowers" means a life dedicated to the arts:

月をめて　花を見つくし　七十三
tsuki o mete hana o mitsukushi nanajūsan
loving the moon / absorbing flowers in her eyes, / at seventy-three

asagao ya
mada tomoshibi no
kage mo ari

morning glory–
shadow of a lantern
still seen

牽牛花<ruby>あさがお</ruby>や
まだ灯火<ruby>ともしび</ruby>の
影<ruby>かげ</ruby>も有<ruby>あり</ruby>

kigo: asagao (morning glory)

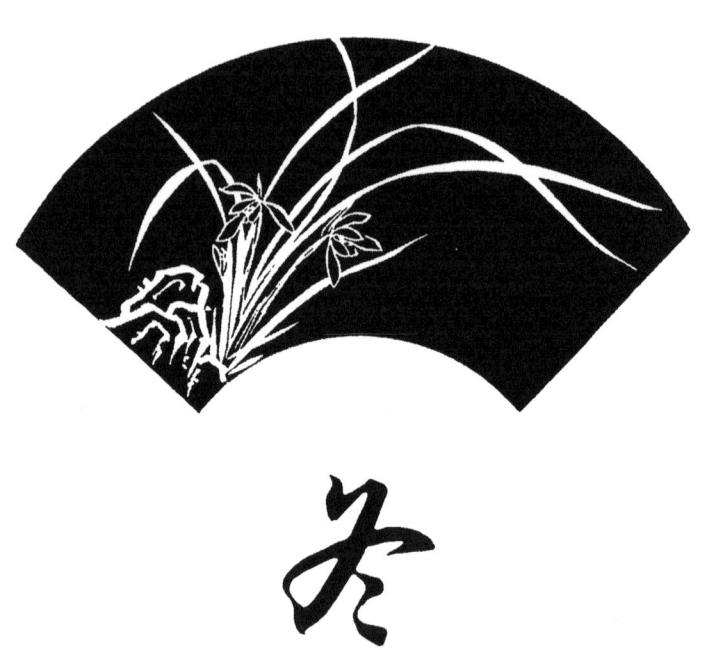

meigetsu ya
yuki fumi wakete
ishi no oto

full moon–
stepping through the snow
the sound of the stones

名月や
雪踏分て
石の音

kigo: meigetsu (full moon) and *yuki* (snow). This poem is usually listed under the autumn *kigo* (full moon), but we choose to list it under the winter *kigo* (snow).

Note: In the silence of the moonlit night, Chiyo-ni hears the sound of *geta* or wooden clogs hitting the stone path beneath the snow.

hatsu shigure
doko yara take no
asaborake

first winter rain–
the bamboo somewhere
in the dawn

はつしぐれ
何所_{どこ}やら竹_{たけ}の
朝朗_{あさぼらけ}

kigo: hatsu shigure (first winter rain)

Note: A haiku which expresses the aesthetic appreciation of hearing the distant or imagined sound of rain on the bamboo.

shiguraru ya
hitoma ni kinō
kyō mo kure

winter rain—
in one room
yesterday, today passes

時雨るゝや
一間にきのふ
けふもくれ

kigo: shigure/shigururu (winter rain)

fuku kaze no
hanare-banare ya
fuyu kodachi

the blowing wind
split, split by
winter trees

吹風の
はなればなれや
ふゆ木立

kigo: fuyu kodachi (winter trees)

oshi wa mata
hitori nagare ka
hatsu shigure

why does the mandarin duck
float alone—
first winter rain

をしはまた
独<ruby>ひとり</ruby>ながれか
初<ruby>はつ</ruby>しぐれ

kigo: hatsu shigure (first winter rain)

Note: Mandarin ducks are always together in pairs and are said to mate for life, so this haiku gives an especially lonely feeling, of the one duck in the freezing rain.

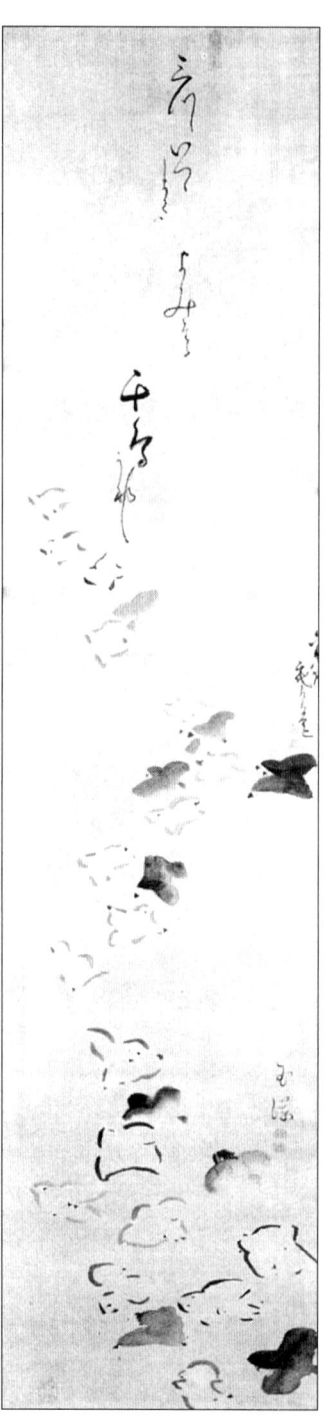

24. *Haiga* with Chiyo-ni's calligraphy of her plover haiku: *mitsu itsutsu / made wa yomitaru / chidori kana* (I can only count / up to three or five– / the plovers), done at age sixty-eight. Illustrated by Gyokuran Ike, a female painter. Matto City Museum.

koe nakuba
sagi ushinawan
kesa no yuki

but for their voices
the herons would disappear–
this morning's snow

声なくば
鷺うしなはむ
今朝の雪

kigo: yuki (snow)

yuki no yo ya
hitori tsurube no
ochiru oto

snowy night—
only the well bucket's
falling sound

雪の夜や
ひとり釣瓶の
落る音

kigo: yuki (snow)

hitorine no
samete shimoyo o
satori keri

sleeping alone
awakened
by the frosty night . . .

独り寝の
さめて霜夜を
さとりけり

kigo: shimoyo (frosty night)

Note: Here the Japanese word *satori* doesn't refer to Zen enlightenment, but rather to something deeply felt or realized.

natsu no yo no
chigiri osoroshi
hashi no shimo

a vow from a summer evening
is frightening–
frost on the bridge

夏の夜の
ちぎりおそろし
橋の霜

kigo: shimo (frost)

Note: The word *chigiri* refers to a lovers' vow.

182

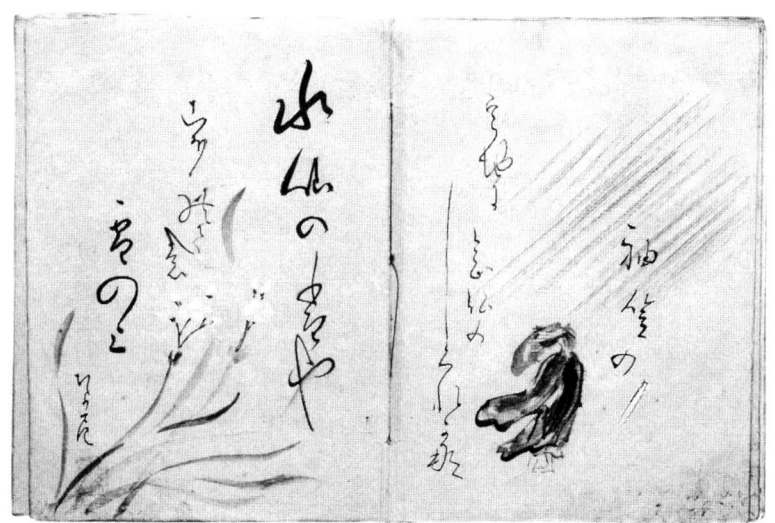

25. One of Chiyo-ni's *haiga* from a notebook, with her naricissus haiku on the left, and one by her haiku teacher Taisui on the right. Matto City Museum.

suisen no
ka ya koborete mo
yuki no ue

narcissus fragrance—
even scattered
over snow

水仙の
香やこぼれても
雪の上

kigo: suisen (narcissus) and *yuki* (snow)

chanohana ya
kono yūgure o
saki nobashi

tea flowers—
their blooming
delays the dusk

茶
の
は
な
や

此
夕
暮
を

咲
の
ば
し

kigo: chanohana (tea flowers)

Note: The tea flower is white, so the light seems to remain on it when night falls.

shinawaneba
naranu ukiyo ya
take no yuki

one must bend
in the floating world–
snow on the bamboo

しなわねば
ならぬ浮世や
竹の雪

kigo: yuki (snow)

Note: In Edo times, the "floating world" (*ukiyo* or *ukinoyo*) referred to everyday life as both a world of instability or transiency and a world of sensuality or pleasure. Closely related is *ukiyoe*, color woodblock prints from the Edo period, which feature kabuki theater scenes, samurai, geisha, pleasure quarters, birds, flowers, and landscapes.

I'm, not shaving my head because I'm rejecting the world, but rather because I feel helpless and lonely thinking about the world of impermanence which is like a stream of water flowing night and day.

kami o yū
te no hima akete
kotatsu kana

putting up my hair
no more—
my hands in the *kotatsu*

髪を結ふ
手の隙あけて
こたつかな

kigo: kotatsu (a hand and foot warmer)

Note: In Chiyo-ni's day, all women had long hair which they put up into elaborate styles. This haiku was written when, at the age of fifty-two, Chiyo-ni became a nun, shaved her head, and changed her name to Soen (Simple Garden). The *kotatsu* is a table covered with a quilt, with a charcoal brazier under it. This haiku shows her relaxation in the freedom that she could now fully live the Way of Haikai.

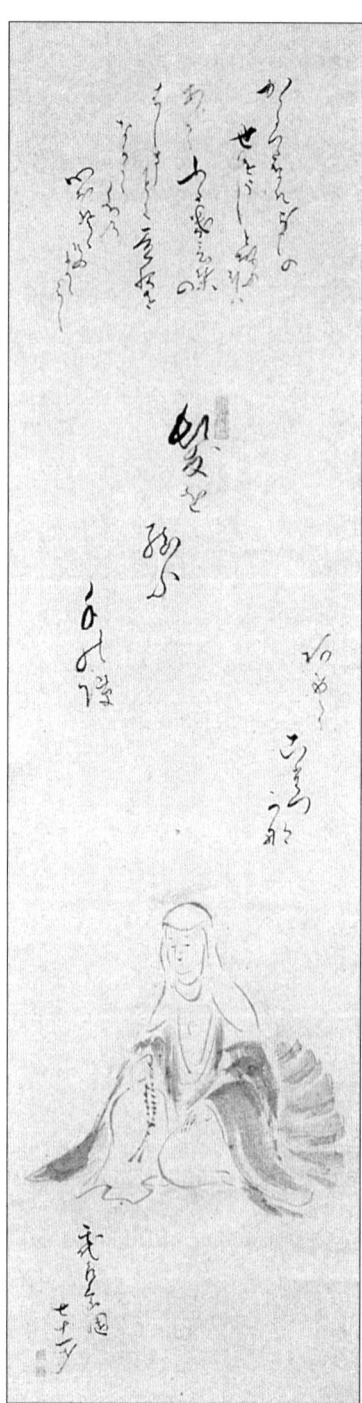

26. This *haiga* is a self-portrait of Chiyo-ni at the age of seventy-one (ca. 1773) with a haiku she had written at age fifty-two on becoming a nun. Keisei Aoki collection, Hakusan, Ishikawa Prefecture, Japan.

Everyone, even the lowest person, is in Amida Buddha's infinite light, so I feel awed and present this grass as an offering.

ha mo chiri mo
hitotsu utena ya
yuki no hana

green leaves or fallen leaves
become one–
in the flowering snow

葉_はも塵_{ちり}も
ひとつ台_{うてな}や
雪_{ゆき}の花_{はな}

kigo: yuki (snow)

Note: Chiyo-ni wrote this while visiting Kyoto's Higashi Honganji temple in March of 1760 to attend Shinran's 500th memorial. This haiku represents Chiyo-ni's deep understanding of Buddhist non-duality.

hachi tataki
yogoto ni take o
okoshikeru

tapping the gourd
every night–
the bamboo is uplifted

鉢<small>はち</small>た
ゝ
き

夜<small>よ</small>毎<small>ごと</small>に竹<small>たけ</small>を

起<small>おこ</small>しける

kigo: hachi tataki (tapping the gourd)

Note: For forty-eight days in winter, the monks of Kūyadō temple in Kyoto went on their rounds every night tapping the gourd with a bamboo stick and reciting the name of Buddha, *Namu Amidabutsu*, as a blessing to all. Perhaps as they walked down the path they compassionately straightened up the bamboo that had blown down or perhaps the bamboo was also awakened by the sound.

nanigoto mo
fude no yukiki ya
fuyu-gomori

all our words
by writing brush–
snowbound

何　筆　冬
事　の　籠
も　往
　　来
　　や

kigo: fuyu-gomori (snowbound)

Note: Another haiku depicting a scene of the snow country:
ころぶ人を　笑ふてころぶ　雪見哉
korobu hito o　warōte korobu　yukimi kana
falling down laughing / at others falling down– / snow viewing

hatsu yuki ya
mono kakeba kie
kakeba kie

first snow—
if I write
it disappears, it disappears

はつ雪や
もの書けば消え
書けば消え

kigo: hatsu yuki (first snow)

Note: This haiku tells about her life as an older writer, when her handwriting revealed her failing health, which was as fragile as the newly fallen snow.

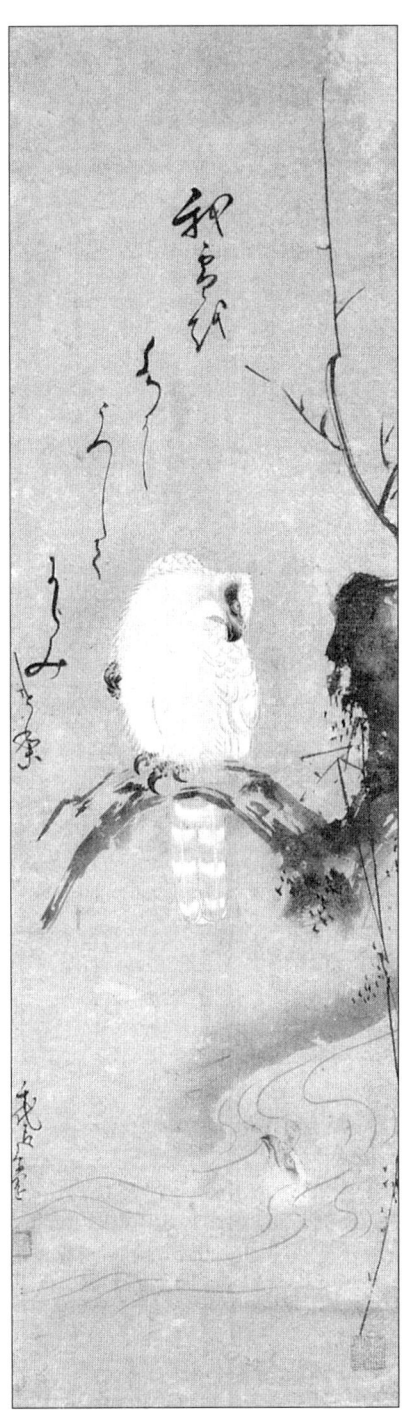

27. A *haiga* with Chiyo-ni's calligraphy, done at around age sixty-four, of her hawk haiku. Illustrated by Shinsei. Matto City Museum.

ware yuki o
mizu ni utsushite
nirami keri

staring
at my snow-white reflection
in the water

我雪を
水にうつして
にらみけり

kigo: yuki (snow)

Note: Another winter hawk haiku:

一枝は　雪ほど鷹に　たはみけり
hito eda wa yuki hodo taka ni tawami keri
the branch / bent by the hawk / as if weighted by snow

Anjin—a settled heart:

> *tomokakumo*
> *kaze ni makasete*
> *kareobana*

> anyway
> leave it to the wind—
> dry pampas grass

ともかくも
風(かぜ)にまかせて
かれ尾(お)花(ばな)

kigo: kareobana (dry pampas grass)

Note: This is one of Chiyo-ni's best-known Buddhist haiku, expressing the peace of detachment.

hana to nari
shizuku to naru ya
kesa no yuki

becoming flowers
becoming water drops–
this morning's snow

花
と
な
り

雫
と
な
る
や

今
朝
の
雪

kigo: yuki (snow)

yuku toshi ya
modokashiki mono
mizu-bakari

the passing year–
irritating things
are only water

行<ruby>ゆく</ruby>としや
もどかしきもの
水<ruby>みずばかり</ruby>斗

kigo: yuku toshi (passing year)

Note: This haiku has a double meaning impossible to translate into English. First, irritating things pass away like flowing water, and second, water is irritating because it is impermanent and always flowing away. This haiku shows Chiyo-ni's human side—that she, too, was sometimes irritated by life's fleeting quality, yet knew that this fact removed the irritating things as well.

197

mono nui ya
yume tatamikomu
shiwasu no yo

sewing things–
I fold in dreams
on a December night

物ぬひや
夢たゝみこむ
師走の夜

kigo: shiwasu (December)

CHIYO-NI'S HAIBUN

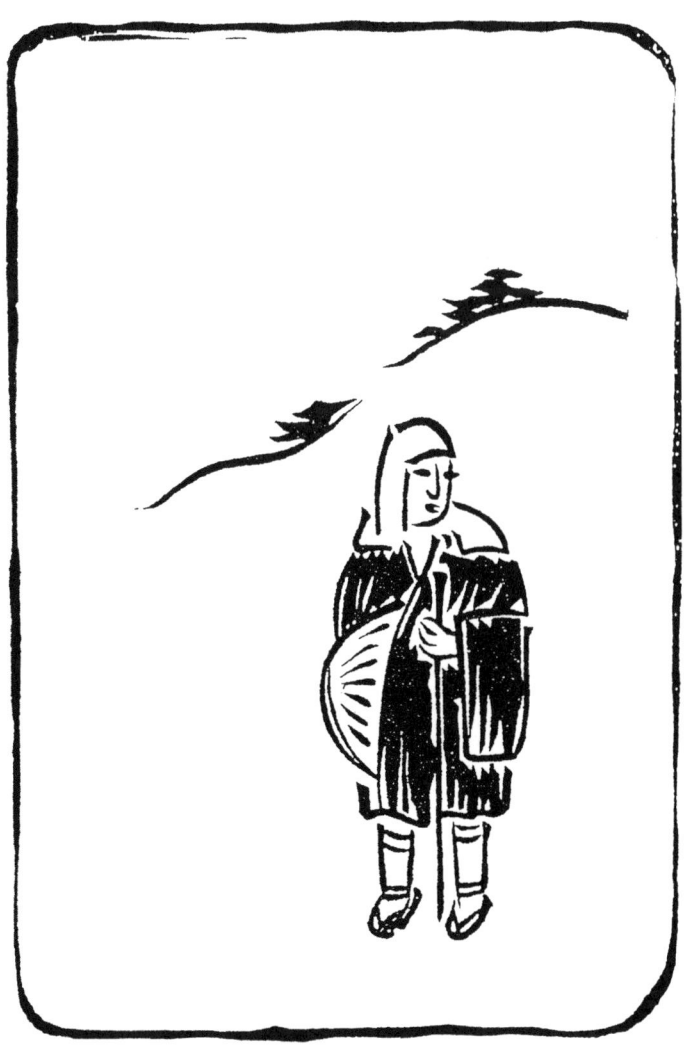

28. A woodblock print by Sakyu Komatsu depicting Chiyo-ni on a pilgrimage, from Nakamoto, *Chiyo-ni no Issho*.

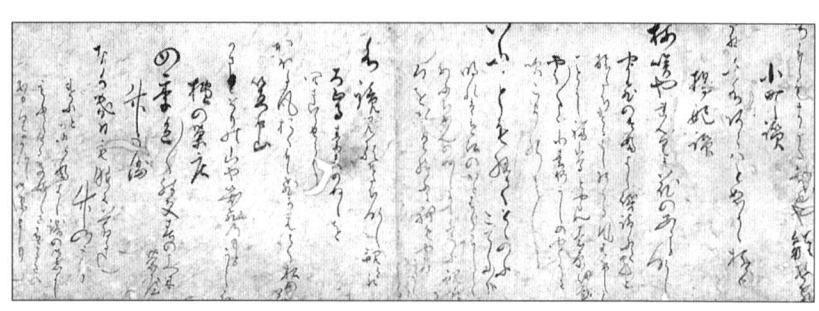

29. *Haibun* (prose and haiku) calligraphy by Chiyo-ni at age sixty on her Yoshizaki journey. Matto City Museum.

PILGRIMAGE TO YOSHIZAKI

吉崎詣 *Yoshizaki Mōde*
1762 (when she was sixty years old)

Around the twentieth of March, when going on a trip to Yoshizaki, the wind was blowing especially hard in Fukushima and Matsubara. So I was relieved to finally reach an inn at Komatsu:

いふことも　羽でととのふ　こてふ哉
iu koto mo　hane de totonou　kochō kana

> what the butterfly*
> wants to say—only this
> movement of its wings

butterfly: Chiyo-ni may be referring to a real butterfly as well as herself here: perhaps she feels tired from her trip so she cannot speak, and perhaps also feels humble so she hesitates to begin writing her *haibun.*

The next morning, I went to Imae-Kata, and close by there I visited a poet who owns Auchi hermitage. After hearing his haiku I was so inspired I couldn't stop making my own haiku:

水鏡　見るそだちなし　蜆取
mizu kagami　miru sodachi nashi　shijimi tori

> rarely looking
> at her reflection in the water–
> the shellfish catcher

Next, I went to visit haijin Sofu at Daishoji temple:

かほる風　おくにひかえて　松の花
kaoru kaze　oku ni hikaete　matsu no hana

> pine flowers*
> in the background–
> the fragrant wind

pine flowers: Chiyo-ni is referring here to Sofu being such a modest poet like the inconspicuous pine flowers.

At Kasatori Mountain I wrote:

かさとりの　山や笑ひも　もどかしき
kasatori no　yama ya warai mo　modokashiki

> Kasatori mountain–
> even becomes green
> slowly

When visiting Tachibana tea house:*

Tachibana: a citrus fruit native to Japan

四季色々　殊更春の　うへ木茶屋
shiki iro-iro　kotosara haru no　ueki chaya

> the four seasons' beauty–
> yet these spring bonsai
> at the teahouse

When sightseeing at Takenoura inlet:

ながき日も　目に暮る也　竹のうら
nagaki hi mo　me ni kururu nari　Takenoura

    Takenoura* inlet–
    even the long spring day
    becomes dark

* *Takenoura:* a wordplay here: the first meaning is the place name for the inlet; the second meaning is "behind the bamboo."

Today I arrived at Yoshizaki for the first time. Because I was so glad I went first of all to the main Buddha hall at the temple to pray:

うつむいた　所が台や　すみれ草
utsumuita　tokoro ga utena ya　sumiresō

    bowing
    at the Buddhist altar–
    the purple violets

Later exploring Kashima:

鶯の　どちらか鳴ぞ　水の影
uguisu no　dochira ka naku zo　mizu no kage

    which warbler
    sings …
    the water's shadow

While viewing Shiogoshi:

しほ越の　松や小蝶は　中もどり
Shiogoshi no　matsu ya kochō wa　naka mo dori

> in mid-flight
> the butterfly returns
> to the pines of Shiogoshi*

*Famous pine trees surrounding the shrine at Shiogoshi that many poets, including Basho, had written about in their travels, as in his *haibun Oku no Hosomichi* (Narrow Road to the Deep North); Chiyo-ni is also referring to herself as the butterfly in this haiku.

After going to the side temple of Yakushi at Yamashiro, as my friends had bid me do, I wrote:*

おのづから　手も地につくや　糸さくら
onozu kara　te mo chi ni tsuku ya　ito zakura

> by themselves also,
> branches touch the ground,**–
> the willowy cherry tree

So having fulfilled my dream to vist Yoshizaki, I headed for home.

*Medicine Buddha, or *Yakushi Ruriko* (Buddha of Emerald Light of the East)

**Implying that they are also bowing down, as if on hands and knees, like Chiyo-ni, in prayer.

CHIYO-NI'S RENGA
LINKED VERSE

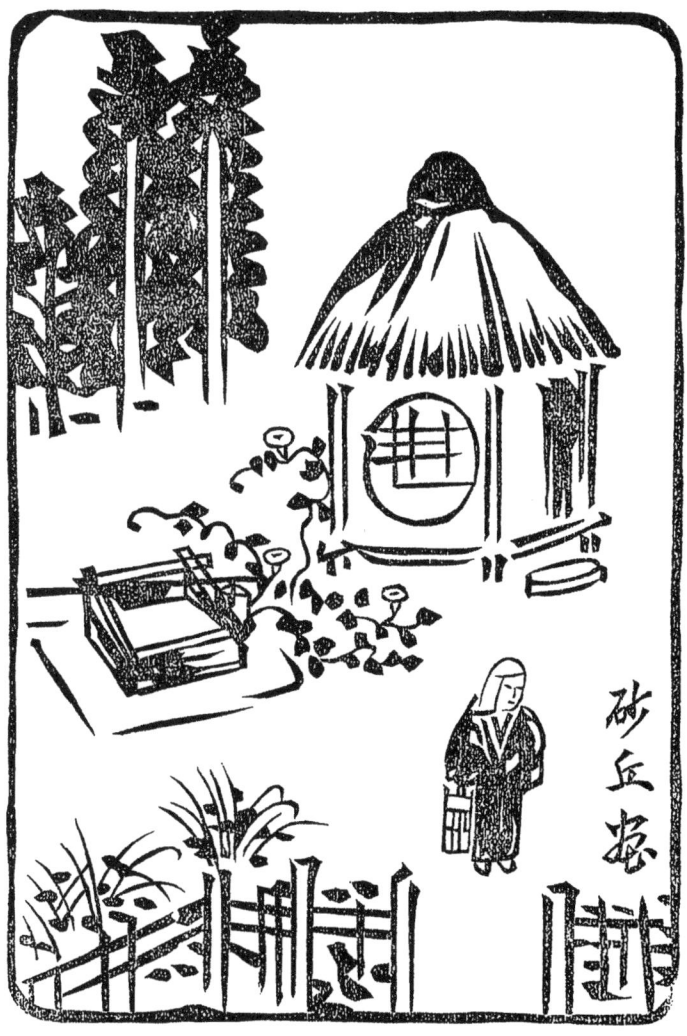

30. A woodblock print by Sakyu Komatsu depicting Chiyo-ni and the backdrop for her most famous morning-glory haiku. From Nakamoto, *Chiyo-ni no Issho*.

It is an autumn night with a full moon. Chiyo-ni and a few of her poet friends gather on the veranda, drink saké or tea, chat and enjoy the moon. Their evening naturally evolves into writing a long poem of linked verse called *renga* (or *renku*, as it has been called in modern times) together. Perhaps they would use the *kigo*, or seasonal reference, of the "full moon" to mark the time of the year and the place, in the *hokku*, or opening verse written as a greeting by the honored guest. This *aisatsu*, or spirit of greeting, as a compliment, blessing, or celebratory toast, was crucial in heralding the *renga* poem.

Such collaborative and improvisational art is an ongoing part of Japanese culture—there is nothing quite like it in the East or West; there are similarities in the linked poetry (*lianju* or *lien-chu*) of China and in the sonnet sequences of the West, but Japanese linked poetry differs by its set number of stanzas, strict rules, alternating authors, and its social function.[1] In East Asia, poetry has always been a social as well as a private activity. However, this kind of social *renga* poetry is unique to Japan.

The haiku, or *hokku* as it was called in Basho's and Chiyo-ni's time, was taken from this *renga* poetry, which at that time was called "*haikai no renga*" (playful linked verse). *Renga* was a form of collaborative poetry originating around the twelfth century, written usually by two or more poets, writing twelve, twenty-four, thirty-six, or one hundred links.

The *renga* form actually evolved from the earlier *tanren-ga*—"dialogue poems," or short linked poems of the tanka court poetry (thirty-one syllables in a five-phrase or five-line poem) from the Heian period (794–1185)—and were often written as a dialogue between friends or lovers. One person would write the first three lines (5-7-5) and the other person would write

Note: The essay on Renga is by Patricia Donegan.

the last two (7-7), completing the poem. Later, in the sixteenth century, the *renga* became less elegant and more lighthearted as more Japanese became literate, which helped to democratize the poetry. However, it was Basho who took the *renga* beyond its light, comic style to express something deeper.[2]

The form of *renga* resembles a cinematic montage, or a collage. There is no continuous narrative: after the *hokku*, starting verse, which marks the poem's occasion and season, there is no temporal order or narrative structure; this is carefully avoided.[3]

"It is more like a mandala," says poet Kris Kondo, "in which the whole range of human experience, as many aspects of life as possible, are included—though without repeating any."[4]

Tadashi Kondo, an expert on *renga* / *renku*, comments:

> In fact, the theory of *renku* as a mandala may not be just metaphorical but historically real. Koyasan and Hase are the two main temples which represent Shingon Esoteric Buddhism in Japan; these two places played an important role in the development of *renga* [*renku*]. ...
>
> The theory states that when you meditate on a mandala, you fuse yourself with it. This means you are aware of every part of it simultaneously, just as during a "*renku* session" you are expected to hold in mind a "*renku* mandala" that contains all the topics, rules and principles, including awareness of the progression of the *renku* so as to know how to complete it. This consciousness is shared among the group so microcosms are integrated into macrocosms of the mandala.[5]

This is meant to accurately reflect the nonduality of the mind and real life, in accord with Buddhist philosophy. Time becomes an eternal moment in which different seasons, places, and ideas are present at the same time, and everything is in flux. This apparent discontinuity, or shifting, is important not only aesthetically, but because it ensures real linking rather than simple expansion.[6] So in *renga* two forces are at work, linking (*tsukeai*) and shifting (*tenji*). The linking connects the adjacent verses, while the shifting generates diversity.[7]

While there are rules which ensure no logical order, at the same time they ensure a structure in the spacing and balancing of images and the emotional tone. These rules, however, vary according to the kind of *renga* written. Generally, each link has a delineated seasonal reference or no seasonal reference; in addition, special topics or images are included a set number of times: love (two to six times); blossom (twice); and the moon (twice). More specifically, the moon, for example, can only be used in, say, link numbers five, fourteen, and twenty-nine. In earlier times, some images, such as the firefly or dragon, could be used only once in a hundred links because they were thought to be too striking. And one strict rule even states that one cannot return to a particular theme with only one verse of another theme in between, to avoid any sense of continuity. The rules, above all, control the tempo of the introduction, development, and close—the quiet beginning, change of direction, climax, and upbeat ending.

The linkage is like a spontaneous conversation: the writer only responds to the lines immediately proceeding, thus creating overlapping poems. This goes back to Nijo Yoshimoto, fourteenth-century *renga* expert, who hinted that *renga* could be a form of meditation because one had to let go of one's preconceptions and just respond spontaneously to what was previously written.[8] So the poet had to be aware of how to link. For example, one of the subtle linking techniques, called *nioi* (fragrance), refers to the mood of one verse imperceptibly drifting into the next, like the fragrance of a flower drifting in the wind.[9]

After a while, however, the rules became so complicated and conservative that people felt stifled and turned to writing the *hokku*, the starting verse (first three lines), more as an independent form, which later became known in the nineteenth century as *haiku*. The *hokku* was appealing because it could be written without paying attention to the bothersome rules of linkage. In Basho's and Chiyo-ni's day, there was little distinction in their minds—*hokku/haiku* was at once an autonomous poem and a verse that could begin a *renga* sequence.[10]

The essence of *renga* is the foundation for the spirit of haiku—a greeting to the world. *Renga* takes people out of their self-centeredness and engages them spontaneously in the present moment. Tadashi Kondo states: "The *renga* makes art a communal dialogue rather than a mere monolgue of one's own self-expression."[11]

For Chiyo-ni and her colleagues, art was more a communal dialogue than not. Although they sometimes worked in solitude, their lives and work attest to how their art was a natural part of their daily social life. *Renga/renku* was and still is a social art, as was haiku in Chiyo-ni's day. Perhaps her vision will be revived in this modern age, which needs a sense of community and cooperation more than ever. Using *renku* and haiku as art in everyday life is a way to accomplish this.

TANRENGA

Today in February, having been invited to this place
                                    —Soen (Chiyo-ni)

賑はひの　ものにすぐれて　ぼたん哉
nigiwai no   mono ni sugurete   botan kana

> in this lively place
> the peony
> most beautiful
>   —Soen (Chiyo-ni)

明やすき夜も　待た朝月
akeyasuki yo mo   habeta asatsuki

> the waning night
> the morning moon awaits
>   —Suejo

Note: This is a *tanrenga* or dialogue/short-linked poem, written between Chiyo-ni and her close friend and disciple Suejo, which reflects the joy and deep intimacy of their relationship.

In mid-February I went down the mountain to Matto; the flowers were in half-bloom; I was so happy to meet this nun living the Way of Haikai

—Chiseki

山に寝し　けがれもゆめか　花の本
yama ni neshi   kegare mo yume ka   hana no moto

under cherry blossoms I wonder
was the dust* from the mountains
but a dream?
—Chiseki

朧押合ふ　中に朝月
oboro oshiau   naka ni asatsuki

in the middle of dense haziness
the morning moon
—Chiyo-ni

Note: In 1765 Chiseki, a young haiku poet, visited Chiyo-ni for the first time. Together they wrote this *tanrenga*, which expresses their joy in meeting each other—as if he came out of a dream, as if she saw the morning moon.

*The word *kegare* is translated here as "dust," and according to Buddhist tradition, literally means "defilement." Perhaps he is showing his humility in coming from the unrefined countryside; he may also be dusty from lodging in the mountains on his way to town to see Chiyo-ni.

"GREETING" HAIKU

Farewell to Gosen

道すがら　清水の種や　けふの雨
michi sugara　shimizu no tane ya　kyō no ame

> on the road
> today's rain
> the seed for clear water

kigo: shimizu (clear water)

Note: This is a farewell haiku written for haiku poet Gosen, the son of *haijin* Kiin (1700–50). Even though it was raining at his departure, it would later become sweet springwater for him to drink on his journey.

Farwell to the fujin, artist

見送れば　墨染に成　花になり
miokureba　sumizome ni nari　hana ni nari

> his departing image
> becomes black-ink kimono
> becomes cherry blossoms

kigo: hana (cherry blossoms)

Note: This is a farewell poem written for poet Kihaku (editor of Chi-yo-ni's poetry collections) in spring of 1760 on his way to Mount Yoshino, famous for cherry blossoms; as he walked away, his kimono image mingled with the cherry trees on the road.

As Gosen goes to Kyoto I lament our separation

蝶ほどの　笠になるまで　したひけり
chō hodo no　kasa ni naru made　shitai keri

till his hat
fades into a butterfly
I yearned for him

kigo: chō (butterfly)

Note: This farewell haiku was written for Gosen in spring of 1770; the use of the words *shitai keri*, meaning "to yearn," gives a more emotional tone than her usual haiku.

Suejo's words are superior to Kyoto's poets

九重の　水はまばゆし　紅の花
kokonoe no　mizu wa mabayushi　beni no hana

Kyoto's water
is dazzling–
yet the rouge flower

kigo: beni no hana (rouge flower)

Note: Chiyo-ni wrote this for her close female friend and disciple Sue-jo (1721–90).

213

For a greeting

取りあへず　塵に敷けり　今朝の雪
toria-e-zu　chiri ni shikikeri　kesa no yuki

> just for now
> I spread the morning's snow
> over the dust

kigo: yuki (snow)

Note: Traditional houses did not have central heating; she probably spread the snow over the earthen floor entrance, so it looked beautiful when her guest came. However, this could possibly be just a metaphor, urging her guest to enjoy the "silver world" of the fresh snow of the north country.

Mourning for Mafu

水仙の　たむけや雪の　眼にわかず
suisen no　tamuke ya yuki no　me ni wakazu

> offering daffodils—
> my eyes can't tell
> which are flowers, which is snow

kigo: suisen (daffodils)

Note: This haiku was written in 1775 on the death of Chiyo-ni's friend and haiku poet, Mafu. She wanted to pick the early spring flowers that were peeking through the snow to offer them at his memorial, but because she was old and couldn't see well, she couldn't find them easily.

Mourning for Plum-Flower Buddha, or the deceased

なごりなごり　散までは見ず　梅の花
nagori nagori　chiru made wa mizu　ume no hana

> sad, so sad
> to miss the plum flower
> before it fell

kigo: ume (plum)

Note: This is a mourning haiku for Shiko (1665–1731), one of Chi-yo-ni's main haiku teachers. "Plum Flower" was one of his pen names. Buddha (*hotoke*) was an honorific name bestowed on the deceased.

Mourning for a lady

そのわかれ　浮草の花　けしの花
sono wakare　ukigusa no hana　keshi no hana

> farewell
> floating flower–
> the red poppy

kigo: keshi no hana (red poppy)

Note: The red poppy can symbolize woman's sensual beauty; Chiyo-ni probably wrote this for the death of a prostitute poet friend.

CHIYO-NI'S RENGA

For Chiyo-jo of Kaga (12 links)
Tai Kayo Chiyo-jo 対加陽千代女

from *Collected Haiku of Chiyo-ni 1764*
Chiyo-ni Ku-shū 千代尼句集

by Chiyo-jo, Otsuyu, and Others
Written at Ise (Mie Prefecture) in 1725
When Chiyo-jo visited haiku master Otsuyu, he invited local haiku
poets and his disciples to gather together and write renku in cele-
bration of her visit.

1. 国の名の　笠に芳はし　花の雪　　　　　麦林
   kuni no na no　kasa ni kaguwashi　hana no yuki

   country name
   on her bamboo hat
   fragrant cherry-blossom snow　　　　　　– Bakurin

2. とをき日影も　水ぬるむころ　　　　　ちよ
   tōki hikage mo　mizu nurumu koro

   distant shadow of the sun
   when the water becomes warm　　　　　– Chiyo

216

3. うぐひすに　雀の朝寝　起されて　　蒼紫
uguisu ni　suzume no asane　okosarete

the sparrow awakened
from its morning sleep
by the nightingale　　　　　　　　　　– Soshi

4. 机の塵を　笑ふ羽箒　　　　　　　　風二
tsukue no chiri o　warau habōki

a feather broom laughing
at the dust on the desk　　　　　　　– Fuji

5. 栗柿に　月下の門の　たのしさよ　東棠
kurigaki ni　gekka no mon no　tanoshisa yo

what a joy
poets with chestnuts and persimmons
under the moon　　　　　　　　　　– Todo

6. 薄着の人に　冬は近よる　　　　奈良　乙峯
usugi no hito ni　fuyu wa chikayoru

winter comes toward　　　　　　　– (Nara)
the ones in light clothes　　　　　　Otomine

7. 雁かねも　乗合せたる　渡し舟　　ちよ
karikane mo　noriawasetaru　watashibune

geese also
ride together
on the ferryboat　　　　　　　　　– Chiyo

8.元三大師　横川ともいう　　　　　　　　麦林
Genzō daishi　Yokawa tomo yū

also called Genzo
Great Master Yokawa　　　　　　　　　　– Bakurin

9.灯を　とぼす間を状の筆とめて　　　　　風二
tomoshibi o　tobosu ma o jō no　fude tomete

while lighting the lantern
she stopped writing letters　　　　　　　– Fuji

10.牡丹の筒も　庭の耶薮から　　　　　　蒼紫
botan no tsutsu mo　niwa no yabu kara

the bamboo holder for peonies
also from a thicket in the garden　　　　– Soshi

11.啼そめる　日和せはしい　蝉の声　　　乙峯
nakisomeru　hiyori sewashii　semi no koe

first cry
on this bustling day–
the cicada's voice　　　　　　　　　　　– Otomine

12.虹も涼しき　紅の乗掛　　　　　　　　東棠
niji mo suzushiki　beni no norikake

the saddle rouge
the rainbow cool　　　　　　　　　　　　– Todo

"Hototogisu"—*renku* (36 links)
(title created by translators, taken from the first three lines)

from *The Princess Ceremony, 1726 (Himenoshiki)* 姫の式
by Chiyo and Shisenjo

Preface to the renku, by the woman haiku poet Shisenjo

The distant sound of a bell is heard. It's a cloudy day in April, 1726. We are enjoying the green leaves, resting from our needle work. Chiyo-ni is visiting me. Since she and I have poles in the same "haiku stream," we wanted to write a *renku* of linked verse about the *hototogisu* [cuckoo], so we went in search of "the first sound of the cloud" (bird in the cloud). After we wrote it, we dedicated our *renku* to the statue of Maya-Bujin (Mother of the Buddha) at Gyozenji temple at Naru, which is known as a women's temple, for assuring safe childbirth.

Preface to the Himenoshiki, *by the editor and haijin Toro*

This temple is famous for the statue of Maya-Bujin (Mother of the Buddha), who saved the three worlds of *san-kai*: realm of desire, realm of form, realm of nonform. Although many women make pilgrimages there to pray for the safe delivery of their children, there is nothing wrong with a man going there, so I went one day to pray at the temple, too. It was there that I noticed a strange haiku-calligraphy scroll dedicated to the temple, so I asked the monk about it, and he said the poets Shisenjo, the wife of someone who lives in Kanazawa, and Chiyo-ni, who lives close by the temple in Matto, had made the *renku* of linked verse. After reading it, I felt a deep sense of *yūgen*, which is like falling petals, or the beauty of falling maple leaves. Each haiku was exquisite, like gold or jade. Because I didn't want the *renku* to remain unknown to others, I asked the monk's permission to publish it. ... In Komatsu there lives another woman *haijin*, Sumajo, so I added her *renku* also, making this a book of three women's *renku*. [Plus haiku by Chiyo-ni, Shisenjo, Sumajo, Kasenjo, and Oku. After it was published, it became known to Shiko and many poets in the haiku world.]

1. 心見の　声ぬれすきな　ほととぎす　　　紫仙女
kokoromi no　koe nuresukina　hototogisu

first cry–
don't be too tearful
cuckoo   – Shisenjo

2. わか葉の雫　宵のむらさめ　　　　　　千代
wakaba no shizuku　yoi no murasame

drops from young leaves
early evening shower   – Chiyo

3. つくばいの　鉢に一波　さざれ来て　　千代
tsukubai no　hachi ni hito nami　sazare kite

a ripple
in the stone bowl
of the garden   – Chiyo

4. 綾の下には　何をめさるゝ　　　　　　紫仙女
aya no shita ni wa　nani o mesaruru

what does she wear
beneath her silk kimono?   – Shisenjo

5. 高々と　色よき鞠の　夕月夜　　　　　　紫仙女
takadaka to　iro yoki mari no　yūzukiyo

up high
a ball of silken colors—*
the moon at dusk　　　　　　　　　　　　—Shisenjo

Mari refers to the ball used in a refined game of football called *kemari*,
introduced from China during the Nara period (710–94) and played by
the nobility. The ball was made of deerskin.

6. 墙の木槿の　両隣から　　　　　　　　　千代
kaki no mukuge　no ryōdonari kara

from both sides
of the autumn flowering hedge　　　　　　—Chiyo

7. 顔見せて　はづすは若い　わたり鳥　　千代
kao misete　hazusu wa wakai　wataridori

face revealed—
missed
the young migrating birds　　　　　　　　—Chiyo

8. 風はあれども　あぶな気のない　　　　　紫仙女
kaze wa aredomo　abunage no nai

there is wind
but no danger　　　　　　　　　　　　　—Shisenjo

9. 船越の　こころもかるふ　ふねの脚　　紫仙女
funagoe no　kokoro mo karū fune no ashi

voyage
with light hearts–
the ship's motion　　　　　　　　　　　　–Shisenjo

10. 焼飯の腹の　無常迅速　　　　　　千代
yaki-ii no hara no　mujō jinsoku*

toasted rice balls–
disappear, so soon　　　　　　　　　　　–Chiyo

*A Buddhist term which refers to the swiftness of transitoriness, and the shortness of life.

11. 暖簾の　しろき御簾屋の　店かへに　　千代
noren no shiroki misuya no misekae ni

white curtain
of the bamboo-shade shop–
the opening　　　　　　　　　　　　　–Chiyo

12. 頬をかかへて　歯医師尋る　　　　紫仙女
hō o kakaete　haishi tazuneru

holding my cheek
I go to the dentist　　　　　　　　　　　–Shisenjo

13. 水仙は　栄耀に花の　咲て居　　　　紫仙女
suisen wa eiyō ni hana no saite ori

daffodils
brilliantly
in bloom　　　　　　　　　　　　　　　−Shisenjo

14. 馬の耳にも　恋の教訓　　　　　　　千代
uma no mimi ni mo koi no kyōkun

lesson of love
whispered in the ear of a horse　　　−Chiyo

15. いのらばや　やすふかなへる十二燈　千代
inoraba ya　　yasū kanaeru jūni tō

prayers−
easily fulfilled
with twelve lanterns　　　　　　　　−Chiyo

16. 杉のはやしに　杉の枝折戸　　　　　紫仙女
sugi no hayashi ni sugi no shiorido

in the cedar forest
a cedar gate

　　　　　　　　　　　　　　　　　　−Shisenjo

17. 時は今　あふさきるさに　月と花　　　紫仙女
toki wa ima ausa kirusa ni tsuki to hana

this moment
to come or to go–
the moon and flowers　　　　　　　　　—Shisenjo

18. 雁も名残に　朝寝したやら　　　　　　千代
kari mo nagori ni   asaneshita yara

geese sad to leave–
overslept perhaps　　　　　　　　　　—Chiyo

19. 仕舞たい　火燵に隙を　やりかねる　千代
shimaitai kotatsu ni hima o yarikaneru

desire
to put away the *kotatsu**
not quite yet　　　　　　　　　　　　—Chiyo

*A quilt-covered table with a heater under it.

20. 娘に押を　かくるとし寄　　　　　　紫仙女
musume ni oshi wo   kakuru toshiyori

the old people
pressure their daughters　　　　　　—Shisenjo

21. 乗物に　ちらりと縫の　裾落て　　　　紫仙女
norimono ni chirari to nui no tsuma ochite

from the vehicle
a glimpse–
the bottom of her kimono　　　　　　　—Shisenjo

22. こゝも峠の　うちか日の岡　　　　千代
koko mo tōge no　uchi ka hino-oka

isn't this mountain pass
in Hinoka?　　　　　　　　　　　　　—Chiyo

23. 雨の音を　洗てすゞし　松の蝉　　　千代
ame no oto o　arōte suzushi　matsu no semi

sound of rain
washing, cool–
the pine's cicadas　　　　　　　　　　—Chiyo

24. 瑠璃手の鉢に　水の浅瓜　　　　紫仙女
rurite no hachi ni　mizu no asauri

in the jade-glass bowl
pickled melon in the water　　　　　　—Shisenjo

25. 文台も　料紙も月も　ゆたかにて　紫仙女
fumidai mo　ryōshi mo tsuki mo　yutaka nite

a writing table
paper and the moon–
such richness　　　　　　　　　　　—Shisenjo

26. すゝきの糸も　風にもまるゝ　　　　千代
susuki no ito mo　kaze ni momaruru

strands of pampas grass
entangled in the wind　　　　　　　　–Chiyo

27. 染かねて　片山紅葉　かたおもひ　　千代
somekanete　katayama momiji　kataomoi

half of the mountain
dyed by red maples–
one-sided love　　　　　　　　　　　–Chiyo

28. さる子細から　天窓丸める　　　　紫仙女
saru shisai kara　tenmado marumeru

head shaven
for some reason　　　　　　　　　–Shisenjo

29. ひたすらに　酒の精進　ばかりなり　紫仙女
hitasura ni　sake no shōjin　bakari nari

devotion
solely
to saké　　　　　　　　　　　　–Shisenjo

30. 小春の空の　暮れやすふなり　　　千代
koharu no sora no　kureyasū nari

Indian summer sky
darkens easily　　　　　　　　　　–Chiyo

31. 四つふたつ　雪の烏の　ころも川　　千代
yotsu futatsu　yuki no karasu no　Koromogawa

two, four*
crows in the snow–
Koromo river　　　　　　　　　　　　　　–Chiyo

*Even numbers, especially four, homophonous in Japanese with the word for "death," are inauspicious in Japan. Odd numbers are preferred, so four here sounds ominous.

32. 一かたまりに　帰る梵論々々　　紫仙女
hitokatamari ni　kaeru boroboro

a group of begging monks
returning　　　　　　　　　　　　　　–Shisenjo

33. 蕎麦切の　山葵に鼻を　はぢけとや　紫仙女
sobagiri no　wasabi ni hana o　hajike to ya

soba noodles
with wasabi*
burn the nose　　　　　　　　　　　　–Shisenjo

wasabi: hot, Japanese horseradish

34. ふるい座敷の　畳あかるい　　　　　千代
furui zashiki no   tatami akarui

in an old room
bright tatami*

　　　　　　　　　　　　　　　　　　−Chiyo

tatami:: thick woven rush mats (six by three feet) used to cover floors
in traditional Japanese houses

35. 見んつりと　花の化粧の　朝かすみ　千代
mintsuri to   hana no keshō no   asakasumi

looking through
the morning mist−
flowers' make-up

　　　　　　　　　　　　　　　　　　−Chiyo

36. 柳に　あそぶ　鳥の百色　　　　　紫仙女
yanagi ni   asobu   tori no momoiro

playing in the willow−
birds of a hundred colors

　　　　　　　　　　　　　　　　　−Shisenjo

"The Middle of a Dream"—*renku* (12 Links)
(title created by translators, taken from the first three lines)

from *Complete Works of Chiyo of Kaga*
Kaga No Chiyo Zenshū 加賀の千代全集 edited by Nakamoto

by Chiyo-ni and Suejo, 1755
Written after Chiyo-ni became a nun and used her Buddhist name,
Soen.

1. 朝かほや　見たらぬ夢の　さめどころ　　すえ
   asagao ya　mitaranu yume no　same dokoro

   morning glories–
   awakened
   in the middle of a dream　　　　　　　　　–Sue

2. 月はながさず　庭の遣水　　　　　　　　素園
   tsuki wa nagasazu　niwa no yarimizu

   not letting the moon float away　　　　　–Soen
   the stream in the garden

3. わたり鳥　むつかしいほど　出ありきて　素園
   wataridori　mutsukashii hodo　dearikite

   migrating birds
   wander about
   noisily　　　　　　　　　　　　　　　　–Soen

229

4. こえかけられて　どちへ行人　　　　　すえ
koe kakerarete　dochi e yuku hito

she is asked
which way she is going　　　　　　　　　—Sue

5. 数足らぬ　舟の竈の　いそがしき　　　すえ
kazu taranu　fune no kamado no　isogashiki

there are not
enough ovens on the boat
so busy　　　　　　　　　　　　　　—Sue

6. 暮たではない　これは雨雲　　　　　　素園
kureta dewanai　kore wa amagumo

it wasn't darkness
but rain clouds　　　　　　　　　　　—Soen

7. 読さして　ひかる源氏も　箱の内　　　素園
yomisashite　hikaru genji mo　hako no uchi

Tale of Genji*
half read
in the box　　　　　　　　　　　　　—Soen

*The world's first novel by the Japanese woman writer Murasaki Shikibu of the tenth century.

8. 火燵のすそを　のぞくから猫　　　　　すえ
kotatsu no suso o　nozoku karaneko

a Chinese cat peeks under
the *kotatsu* cover   —Sue

9. ひとつづつ　かぜからちがふ　鐘の声　すえ
   hitotsu zutsu   kaze kara chigau   kane no koe

each sound of
the temple bell is different
in the wind   —Sue

10. 都はなれて　恋も古びる　　　　　　　素園
    miyako hanarete   koi mo furubiru

away from Kyoto
love also gets old   —Soen

11. 花の名は　袖からもれて　伽羅の音　すえ
    hana no na wa   sode kara morete   kyara no oto

the name of the flower
wafts from her sleeves:
scent of aloeswood*   —Sue

*This is a reference to *kōdō*, an incense-listening game from the courtly
arts period (Heian: 794–1185), an aesthetic still practiced in modern
times. Here, the scent of incense wafts from her sleeves because kimo-
nos were sometimes stored with incense, and the scent remained in the
clothing even when worn.

12. むすびもながく　枝折戸の藤　　　　　素園
    musubi mo nagaku   shiorido no   fuji

long ending ties
wisteria by the wicker gate   —Soen

clear water is cool
fireflies vanish–
there's nothing more

I also saw the moon
and so I say goodbye
to this world

NOTES

PREFACE

1. R. H. Blyth, *A History of Haiku*, vol. 1. (Tokyo: Hokuseido Press, 1963–64), p. 223, p. 34.

CHIYO-NI'S LIFE

1. Jodo Nakamoto, ed., *Kaga no Chiyo Zenshu* (Complete Works of Chiyo of Kaga) (Kanazawa: Hokkoku Publishing Co., 1983), p. 1.
2. Chie Nakane and Oishi Shinzaburo, eds., Conrad Totman, trans., *Tokugawa Japan: The Social and Economic Antecedents of Modern Japan* (Tokyo: University of Tokyo Press, 1990), p. 119.
3. Tadashi Yamane, *Matto no Haijin Chiyo-jo* (Matto's Poet Chiyo-jo) (Matto: Matto City), pp. 25–26.
4. Kanajo Hasegawa, *Kaga no Chiyo* (Chiyo of Kaga) (Tokyo: Shiki Shuppan, 1986), pp. 39–40.
5. Charles Dunn, *Everyday Life in Traditional Japan* (Tokyo: Charles E. Tuttle Co., 1969), pp. 170–172.
6. Nakamoto, *Kaga no Chiyo Zenshu*, p. 547.
7. *Zoku Kinsei Kijinden* (Famous People of the Edo Period), vol. 2, (1798), quoted in Nakamoto, *Kaga no Chiyo Zenshu*, p. 547.
8. Ibid., pp. 46–50.
9. Makiko Bessho, *Bashō ni Hirakareta Haikai no Joseishi—Rokuju Rokunin no Komachi Tachi* (Women's History of Haiku Opened by Bashō—Sixty-Six Women) (Tokyo: Origin Shuppan Center, 1993), pp. 183–84.
10. Ranko, afterword, *Chiyo-ni Kushu* (Haiku Collection of Chiyo the Nun).
11. Tadashi Yamane, *Matto no Haijin Chiyo-jo* (Matto's Poet Chiyo-jo) (Matto: Matto City), pp. 65–70.
12. Tsuyu Kawashima, *Joryu Haijin* (Women Haiku Poets) (Tokyo: Meiji Shoin, 1957), pp. 134–37.
13. Nakamoto, *Kaga no Chiyo Zenshu*, p. 555.

14. Ibid., p. 43.
15. Hasegawa, *Kaga no Chiyo*, pp. 40–49.
16. Nakamoto, *Kaga no Chiyo Zenshu*, p. 1.
17. Fujie Yamamoto, "Kaga no Chiyo," in *Nihon no Joseishi* (History of Japanese Women), vol. 4 (Tokyo: Shueisha, 1974), p. 286.
18. Jodo Nakamoto, *Chiyo-ni no Issho* (The Life of Chiyo-ni) (Matto: Committee for 150th Commemoration of Chiyo-ni, 1935), p. 6.
19. Hasegawa, *Kaga no Chiyo*, pp. 49–51.
20. Yamane, *Matto no Haijin Chiyo-jo*, pp. 47–48.
21. Kawashima, *Joryu Haijin*, pp. 148–150.
22. Ibid., p. 150.
23. Ibid., pp. 138–39.
24. Yamamoto, "Kaga no Chiyo," pp. 284–86.
25. Ibid., p. 284.
26. Hasegawa, *Kaga no Chiyo*, p. 76.
27. Nakamoto, *Zenshu*, pp. 588–89.
28. Hasegawa, *Kaga no Chiyo*, pp. 53–54.
29. Ibid., pp. 50–60.
30. Joyce Lebra, et al, eds., *Women in Changing Japan* (Boulder: Westview Press, 1976), passim.
31. Yamane, *Matto no Haijin Chiyo-jo*, p. 85.
32. Hasegawa, *Kaga no Chiyo*, p. 58.
33. Yamane, *Matto no Haijin Chiyo-jo*, p. 87.
34. John M. Rosenfield, *The Courtly Tradition in Japanese Art and Literature* (Tokyo: Kodansha, 1973), p. 123.
35. Authors' interview of Master Osamu Nakano, abbot of Shokoji temple, Matto, November 19, 1994.
36. To-shoin, Preface to *Chiyo-ni Kushu* by Chiyo-ni.
37. Hisao Inagaki, *Dictionary of Japanese Buddhist Terms* (Kyoto: Nagata Bunshodo, 1984), pp. 157, 167, 335; reference to the *Kanmuryo-ju-kyo*: meditation of the Buddha of Infinite Light Sutra called *Ju-rokkan*, "The Sixteen Contemplations on Amida Buddha."
38. Chogyam Trungpa Rinpoche, *Cutting Through Spiritual Materialism* (Berkeley: Shambhala Publishers, Inc., 1973), p. 225.
39. Nakamoto, *Chiyo-jo no Issho*, pp. 61–63.
40. Yamane, *Matto no Haijin Chiyo-jo*, p. 77.

41. Ibid., pp. 75–77.

42. Jodo Nakamoto, ed., *Shinseiki-shu* (A Collection of Chiyo-ni's Original Paintings) (Kanazawa: Hokkoku Publishers, 1983), p. 176.

43. Yamane, *Matto no Haijin Chiyo-jo*, p. 76.

44. Nakamoto, *Kenkyu*, p. 247.

45. Hasegawa, *Kaga no Chiyo*, p. 27.

46. Yamane, *Matto no Haijin Chiyo-jo*, p. 64.

47. Donald Keene, *Dawn to the West: Japanese Literature of the Modern Era, Poetry, Drama and Criticism* (New York: Holt, Rinehart and Winston, 1976), p. 134.

48. Miwata Gendo, ed., *Nihon Josei Bunka Shi*, vol. 2 (Japanese Women's Poetry) (Tokyo: Zenkoku Koto Gakko-Cho Kyokai, 1938–39), p. 614.

49. Kawashima, *Joryu Haijin,* p. 6.

50. Ibid.

51. Nakamoto, *Zenshu,* pp. 656–693.

52. Hasegawa, *Kaga no Chiyo,* p. 94.

53. Ibid.

54. Nakamoto, *Zenshu,* p. 114.

55. Nakamoto, *Zenshu,* pp. 539–42.

56. Ibid.

57. Yamamoto, "Kaga no Chiyo," p. 248.

58. Hasegawa, p. 58.

THE HAIKU FORM

1. Arthur Waley, *Japanese Poetry: The Uta* (Honolulu: University of Hawaii Press, 1976), introduction.

2. Teijo Nakamura, article in *Libre Magazine* (Tokyo: Liberal Democratic Party, February 1986), p. 42.

3. Seishi Yamaguchi, *Haiku Tensaku Kyoshitsu* (Haiku Correction Class Study) (Tokyo: Tokyo University Press, 1986), introduction.

4. Donald Keene, *World Within Walls: Japanese Literature of the Pre-Modern Era, 1600–1867* (New York: Grove Press, Inc., 1976), p. 89.

5. Donald Keene, *Japanese Literature: An Introduction for Western Readers* (New York: Grove Press, 1955), pp. 40–41.

6. Toshiharu Oseko, *Bashō's Haiku: Literal Translations for Those Who Wish to Read the Original Japanese* (Tokyo: Maruzen Co., Ltd., 1990), introduction. See term: b. *"mono no mie-taru hikari"* under 4. "Bashō's Haiku & His Cultural Background."

7. Kenkichi Yamamoto, "Aisatsu to Kokkei" (Greeting and Humor) in *Junsui Haiku* (Pure Haiku) (Tokyo: Sogensha Publishers, 1952).

8. Shuson Kato, Atsugo Otani, Noichi Imoto, eds., *Haibungaku Daijiten* (Haiku Literature Dictionary) (Tokyo: Kadokawa Shoten, 1995), p. 1.

9. Conrad Totman, *Early Modern Japan* (Berkeley: University of California Press, 1993), p. 406.

10. Keene, *World Within Walls,* p. 339.

11. Ibid., p. 143. The list of Bashō's ten main disciples vary according to the critic, but usually include: Kikaku, Ransetsu, Kyorai, Naito Joso, Kyoriku, Shiko, Shida Yaba, Tachibana Hokushi, Sugiyama Sampu, and Ochi Etsujin; and sometimes also Nozawa Boncho and Kawai Sora.

12. Minoru Horikiri, *Bashō no Monjin* (Disciples of Bashō). (Tokyo: Iwanami Shoten, 1991), pp. 183–84.

13. Makota Ueda, *Literary and Art Theories in Japan* (Cleveland: Western Reserve University Press, 1967), p. 166.

14. Keene, *World Within Walls,* p. 116.

15. Horikiri, p. 175.

16. Keene, *World Within Walls,* pp. 124–25.

17. Bessho, p. 187.

18. Gyofu Soma, "Kaga no Chiyo" (Chiyo of Kaga) in *Teishin to Chiyo to Rengetsu* (Tokyo: Shunjusha, 1930), pp. 108–112.

19. Nakamoto, *Chiyo-ni Zenshu,* p. 7.

20. Kawashima, *Joryu Haijin,* p. 130.

21. Ibid., p. 257.

22. Ueno, p. 38.

23. Nakamoto, *Kaga no Chiyo Zenshu,* p. 655.

24. To-shoin, preface to *Chiyo-ni Ku-shu* (Haiku Collection of Chiyo the Nun), Mugaian Kihaku, ed. (Kyoto: Ko-to Tachibanaya Jihei, 1764).

25. Oseko, *Bashō's Haiku.* See term: a.1, *"matsu no koto wa, matsu ni narae."*

26. Kenneth Yasuda, *The Japanese Haiku: Its Essential Nature, History and Possibilities in English with Selected Examples.* (Tokyo: Charles E. Tuttle Co., 1957), pp. 24, 31.

27. Tadashi Yamane, "Kaga no Chiyo Hitogara to Kufu Hairon" (Character of Chiyo-ni and Her Haiku Style) in *Kyodo to Bunka,* vol. 4 (Matto: Matto City, 1977), p. 37.

28. Shoin, preface to *Chiyo-ni Ku-shu* (Haiku Collection of Chiyo the Nun), Mugaian Kihaku, ed. (Kyoto: Koto Tachibanaya Jihei, 1764).

29. Nakamoto, *Chiyo-ni Zenshu,* p. 7.

30. Authors' interview with Suzuko Shinagawa, April 17, 1995, Osaka, Japan.

31. Donald Keene, *Dawn to the West: Japanese Literature of the Modern Era—Poetry, Drama and Criticism.* (New York: Holt, Rinehart and Winston, 1976), p. 134.

32. Takahama Kyoshi, *Haiku Dokuhon* (Haiku Book) (Tokyo: Shinju Publishing Co., 1977), pp. 133–42.

33. Ibid.

34. Authors' interview with Osamu Nakano, abbot of Shokoji temple, October 19, 1994, Matto City, Japan.

35. Kyoshi, *Haiku Dokuhon,* pp. 133–42.

36. D. T. Suzuki, *Zen and Japanese Culture* (New York: Princeton University Press, 1959), pp. 245–46.

37. Suzuki, quoted in Robert Aitken, *A Zen Wave: Bashō's Haiku and Zen* (New York and Tokyo: Weatherhill, Inc., 1978), p. 77.

38. Suzuki, *Zen and Japanese Culture,* p. 247.

39. Aitken, pp. 77–78.

40. Kawashima, *Joryu Haijin,* p. 141.

41. Makiko Bessho, *Kotoba o Te ni Shita Shisei no Onna-tachi* (Ordinary Women Who Acquired Words) (Tokyo: Origin Shuppan Center, 1993), p. 4.

42. Kawashima, *Joryu Haijin,* p. 149.

43. Ibid.

RENGA (LINKED VERSE)

1. *Kodansha Encyclopedia of Japan,* vol. 4 (Tokyo: Kodansha Ltd., 1983), p. 296.

2. Ueda, *Bashō and His Interpreters: Selected Hokku with Commentary* (Stanford: Stanford University Press, 1992), p. 1.

3. Elizabeth Mayhew, *The Monkey's Raincoat: Linked Poetry of the Bashō School with Haiku Selections* (Tokyo: Charles E. Tuttle Company, 1985), p. 31.

4. Kris Kondo, "Renku in the Classroom" in *Iiyama Memoirs* vol. 13, no. 1 (Tokyo: Women's Junior College, Tokyo Institute of Polytechnics), p. 104.

5. Tadashi Kondo, *Haiku and Renku Reunited* (Tokyo: Seikei University, 1994), p. 43.

6. Bill Higginson, *International Linked Poetry and the Japanese Tradition* (New York: Haiku Society of America, Inc., 1993), p. 1.

7. Bill Higginson and Tadashi Kondo, *Link and Shift: A Practical Guide to Renku Composition* (Tokyo: Seikei University, 1994), pp. 116–17.

8. Ueda, *Literary and Art Theories in Japan,* pp. 52–53.

9. Ueda, *Bashō and His Interpreters,* p. 428.

10. Ibid., p. 3.

11. Interview of Tadashi Kondo by Patricia Donegan, Tsurumaki, Japan, 1995.

CHIYO-NI'S HAIKU LINEAGE TREE
千代女関係俳人系図

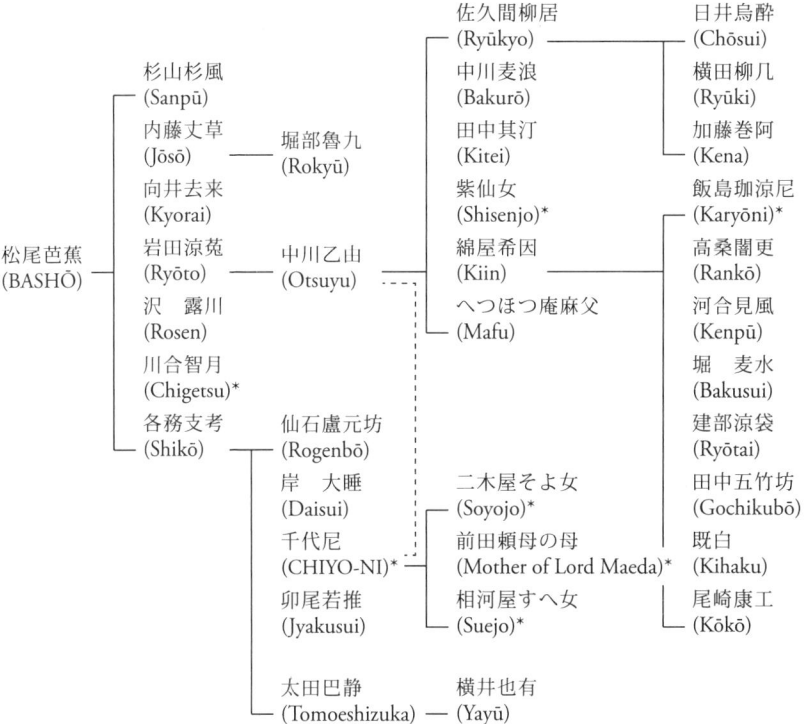

*denotes a female *haijin*

Note: This lineage tree was adapted from the book *Matto no Haijin Chiyo-jo* by Tadashi Yamane. A longer list of Bashō's ten disciples is on page 231, fn 11.

Glossary

"ah!" or *haiku moment:* This is not a Japanese term, but does relate to Basho's theory of becoming one with nature, a moment of heightened awareness when one is present to the moment and forgets the self—a state thought important by some to write good haiku. The term is used mostly by Westerners like R. H. Blyth and Japanese scholars like D. T. Suzuki, to explain the Zen perspective of haiku to non Japanese.

aisatsu/aisatsu no ku: the spirit of greeting/haiku as a greeting

aware: "Sad-beauty" or pathos, is an aesthetic from the Heian (794–1185), meaning something that is transient as well as beautiful (i.e., plum blossoms).

dō: or *michi*; the Way, or path; *tao* in Chinese

fūga/fūryū: In Basho's time, this referred to artistic refinement in one's life and art; *fūga no michi* referred to following the Way of Elegance, or Way of an art form like *haikai*, flower arranging, tea ceremony, etc. If only referring to haiku, *haikai no michi* was usually used.

haibun: Combination of prose interspersed with *hokku* or haiku, usually recording a journey; Basho's long *Oku no Hosomichi* (Narrow Road to the Deep North) and Chiyo-ni's *Yoshizaki Mōde* (Pilgrimage to Yoshizaki) are examples of this form.

haiga: combined painting with a haiku or other calligraphic writing

haijin: professional or master haiku poet living the Way of Haikai

haikai: abbreviation of *haikai no renga* (linked verse); form of *renga* opposed to traditional elegant *renga*; originally a classification of humorous poems; also a general term for all types of literature stemming from *haikai no renga* including *hokku*, haiku, and *haibun*

haikai no michi: following the Way of Haiku in daily life; espoused by Basho

haikai no renga: umbrella term for all linked verse; usually known as *renga* or *renku*

haiku: abbreviation of *haikai no ku*; Japanese independent verse form normally having a seventeen (or 5-7-5) syllable pattern or three lines in English, and containing a *kigo*, or seasonal word, and a recording of a heightened moment. Haiku is a poetry of the common people, whereas the earlier tanka poetry was a poetry of the nobility; strictly speaking, only verse written in the modern period (since 1868) should be called haiku.

hokku: Opening verse (5-7-5) of a *renga/renku* sequence, having seventeen syllables and a seasonal word. In the Edo period (1603–1867) it began to be appreciated as a verse form independent from the rest of the sequence; in the late nineteenth century when linked verse waned, *hokku* became a completely independent form known as *haiku.*

hon-i: heart of things, often a *kigo,* or seasonal reference, evoking emotion of the thing itself

hosomi: slenderness or sparseness of expression—a Basho aesthetic

ichi-go-ichi-eh: "Appreciation of this moment's one meeting"; the term originated in Buddhism and was later used in the tea ceremony, especially by tea-master Rikyu (1522–91).

jisei no ku: death poem written right before one's death

kadō: the Way of Poetry (referring to *tanka/waka* court poetry); from the Japanese arts tradition of the Kamakura period (1186–1336) on; one of the ways believed to lead to enlightenment

kakejiku: scroll painting of a scene or calligraphy

kakekotoba: pivot-word; a kind of pun, a word with a double meaning pivoting in two directions, both to the previous word and to the following word (see haiku on pp. 149)

karumi: Simplicity or lightness; a style without artifice that records the beauty of simple things. Examples from Basho's last theory of haiku—"eat vegetable soup rather than duck soup," "be light as a shallow river flowing over a sandy bed," and "observe what children do."

kasen: the 36 links of a *renga* (linked verse) sequence; sometimes 18 links, or *hankasen*

kidai: Broad seasonal topic; for example a group of haiku/*waka* poets agrees to write on a topic, like say, the moon. In the *saijiki* or *kigo* dictionary there are subtopics under the broad seasonal topic—for example, under the *kidai* of the moon there are *kigo* listed: emerging moon, crescent moon, hesitant moon, hazy moon, 16th night moon, arc moon, etc.

kigo: Specific seasonal reference (e.g., morning glory) designating the season of a haiku, the emotional tone, and cultural associations; in Chiyo-ni's time, sometimes double *kigo* or more were used, so modern scholars categorize the haiku according to what they feel is the "strongest" *kigo.*

kireji: Japanese "cutting word" indicating a break or stop, such as *ya, keri, kana. Ya* indicates an emphatic pause and divides the haiku into two parts (usually indicated in English by a colon, dash or exclamation point). *Keri* adds emotion to the preceding verb and marks a pause. *Kana* gives emphasis to the word preceding it, with an emotional effect like a soft sigh, usually marking the end of a haiku. Since the traditional Japanese language used virtually no punctuation, *kireji* may have their origins in that fact. Sometimes punctuation marks are used by translators to delineate *kireji*—which is a better approach than trying to explain the emotion; however, *kireji* themselves remain almost untranslatable.

kyakkan byōsha: objectivity—the method of writing haiku in an objective way; a concrete description with little or no comment or emotion expressed; modern haiku poet Shiki's interpretation of Basho's view of writing haiku

makoto: sincerity, honesty, or truth; ideal of poetry espoused by Basho

mono no aware: shortened sometimes to *aware,* an aesthetic from the Heian period (794–1185) on; the beauty of the ephemeral, "sad beauty," or poignancy

mujō: "impermanence"; the first noble truth of Buddhism, that everything is transient

mushin: "empty heart"; unattached state of mind (from Buddhism); also sometimes "without heart," meaning nonstandard verse

nioi: fragrance, a subtle linking technique in *renga/renku*

onji: Phonetic symbol or sound symbol, to count a Japanese poem's number of syllables; for example, the long ō is considered to be two syllable counts in Japanese rather than one in English. Thus Bashō has three rather than two syllable counts. Another example, the double consonant is also given a two syllable duration, as in *sakka* (writer), so it is three rather than two syllable counts in Japanese *onji;* knowing this helps one to count the seventeen syllables of a

Japanese haiku.

renga: linked verse written by two or more poets, originating in the Heian period (794–1185), and popularized in the fourteenth century—usually verses of thirty-six or one hundred links, with alternating lines of fourteen (7-7) or seventeen syllables (5-7-5) each; in the sixteenth century a less elegant and more common people's *renga* emerged

renku: modern term for *renga* used since the beginning of the twentieth century to distinguish a more popular form of *renga*

sabi: detached loneliness, espoused by the Basho school

saijiki: seasonal reference dictionary, used by *haijin* (haiku poets) to find the right *kigo,* seasonal reference word

senryū: Satirical/humorous verse form, a variant of haiku, also written in 5-7-5 syllable count; its subject was usually the human or social realm rather than nature.

shasei: On-the-spot sketch from nature/life, especially promoted by the modern poet Shiki Masaoka (1867–1902), although the idea of writing directly from nature was one of Basho's main theories.

shibumi: astringency; the beauty of subdued images

shikishi: a square sheet of beautiful paper or cardboard, to write calligraphy or poetry on

shiori: tenderness, suggestive of delicacy of feeling; a sensitive observation of the human or natural world; espoused by Basho

shizen to hitotsu ni naru: (a literal translation—not a set term in Japanese nor used by Basho); "oneness with nature," an aesthetic espoused by Basho, later written down by his disciple Doho

shōfū: Basho's style; any *haikai* in the styles of Basho in his mature years

shū: collection or anthology of literature

sokkyō: spontaneity; ideal advocated by Basho, though not a set term in Japanese, nor used by Basho

tanka: court poetry of thirty-one syllable count (5-7-5-7-7) or five phrases, at its height in the Heian period (794–1185)

tanrenga: short linked poem or dialogue poem between two people, the first person writing 5-7-5 syllables, or three phrases, and the second person writing the concluding 7-7 syllables, or two phrases, of the verse; popularized in the *tanka* poetry of the court period and still used later as "greeting poems" in the Edo period and following *tanzaku:* long strip of refined paper or cardboard to write a poem or other writing in calligraphy

tokonoma: recessed alcove in the wall of a Japanese house where a scroll painting is hung and a flower arrangement placed

tsukinami: overly common or uninspired poetry

uta-hiza: seated pose to write a poem on one's knee

wabi: poverty of spirit, or the beauty of simple things, especially related to the tea ceremony; an aesthetic of Basho

waka: general term for Japanese poetry; from the Heian-period traditional court verse form of thirty-one syllables of five phrases (5-7-5-7-7); if written in modern times, a *tanka*

Way of Haikai: also known as *haikai no michi* in Japanese; a life wholly devoted to haiku, especially promoted by Basho

yugen: beauty of depth and mystery; an aesthetic especially cultivated in the twelfth to fifteenth centuries in relation to Noh drama

zazen: zen meditation

Bibliography

IN ENGLISH

*Asterisks indicate sources which include translations of Chiyo-ni's haiku.

Ackroyd, Joyce, "Women in Feudal Japan." *Transactions of the Asiatic Society of Japan,* 3rd series, vol. 7, 1959.

Aitken, Robert. *A Zen Wave: Bashō's Haiku and Zen.* New York and Tokyo: Weatherhill, Inc., 1978.*

Akmakigian, Hiag. *Snow Falling from a Bamboo Leaf: The Art of Haiku.* Santa Barbara, CA: Capra Press, 1979.

Aston, William George. *A History of Japanese Literature.* London: 1899.*

Barnstone, Willis and Aliki, eds., *Book of Women Poets from Antiquity to Now.* 1980. Revised edition. New York: Schocken Books, 1993.*

Blyth, R.H. *Haiku,* four volumes. Tokyo: Hokuseido Press, 1949–52.*

____*A History of Haiku,* vols. 1, 2. Tokyo: Hokuseido Press, 1963–64.*

Bowers, Faubion, ed., *An Anthology of Classic Haiku: From Sogi to Shiki.* New York: Dover Publications, Inc., 1997.*

Buchanan, Daniel C. *One Hundred Famous Haiku.* Tokyo: Japan Publications, 1973.*

Carter, Steven D., ed. *Traditional Japanese Poetry: An Anthology.* Stanford, CA: Stanford University Press, 1991.*

Chamberlain, Basil Hall. *A Handbook of Colloquial Japanese.* 3rd edition. Tokyo: Hakubunsha, 1898.*

____"Bashō and the Japanese Poetical Epigram." *Transactions: The Asiatic Society of Japan,* vol. XXX, pp. 243–362. Tokyo: Rikkyo Gakuin Press, 1902.*

____*Japanese Poetry.* London: John Murray, 1910.*

Note: Macrons are used for authors' names and titles of works only.

Cosman, et al., eds. *Penguin Book of Women Poets.* Middlesex, UK: Penguin Books, Ltd., 1978.*

Dunn, Charles J. *Everyday Life in Traditional Japan.* Tokyo: Charles E. Tuttle Company, 1969.

Fister, Patricia. *Japanese Women Artists (1600–1900).* Essay by Fumiko Yamamoto. New York: Harper and Row, 1988.*

Giroux, Joan. *The Haiku Form.* Tokyo: Charles E. Tuttle Company, 1974.

Hamill, Sam. *The Sound of Water: Haiku by Bashō, Buson, Issa, and other Poets.* Boston and London: Shambhala, 1995.*

Hass, Robert. *Essential Haiku (Versions of Bashō, Buson, and Issa).* Hopewell, New Jersey: Ecco Press, 1994.

Hearn, Lafcadio. *In Ghostly Japan.* Boston: Little, Ltd., 1899. Tokyo: Charles E. Tuttle Company, 1971.*

Henderson, Harold. *An Introduction lo Haiku: An Anthology of Poems and Poets from Bashō to Shiki.* New York: Anchor Books, 1958.*

Higginson, William J. *The Haiku Handbook.* New York: McGraw-Hill, 1985.*

_____ *The Haiku Seasons: Poetry of the Natural World.* Tokyo: Kodansha International, 1996.

_____ *Haiku World: An International Poetry Almanac.* Tokyo: Kodansha International, 1997.

_____ *International Linked Poetry and the Japanese Tradition.* New York: Haiku Society of America, Inc., 1993.

Higginson, William J. and Tadashi Kondo. *Link and Shift: A Practical Guide to Renku Composition.* Tokyo: Seikei University, 1994.

Hla-Dorge, Gilberte. *Une Póetesse Japonaise au XVIII siecle, Kaga no Tchiyo-jo.* Paris: Maisonneuve, 1936 (in French).*

Hoffman, Yoel, ed. and trans. *Japanese Death Poems: Written by Zen Monks and Haiku Poets On the Verge of Death.* Tokyo: Charles E. Tuttle Company, 1986.*

Kato, Koko, ed. *Four Seasons: Haiku Anthology Classified by Season Words in English and Japanese.* Tokyo: Ko Poetry Association, 1991.

Keene, Donald. *Dawn to the West: Japanese Literature of the Modern Era: Poetry, Drama, Criticism.* New York: Holt, Rinehart and Winston, 1984.

_____ *Japanese Literature: An Introduction for Western Readers.* New York: Grove Press, 1955.

_____ *World Within Walls (Japanese Literature of the Pre-Modern Era, 1600–1867).* New York: Grove Press, 1976.*

Kodaira, Takashi, and Alfred H. Marks, trans. *The Essence of Modern Haiku: 300 Poems by Seishi Yamaguchi.* Atlanta: Mangajin Books, 1993.

Kondo, Kris. "Renku in the Classroom." *Iiyama Memoirs,* vol. 13, no. 1. Tokyo: Women's Junior College, Tokyo Institute of Polytechnics, 1996.

Kondo, Tadashi, and William J. Higginson, trans. *Red Fuji: Selected Haiku of Yatsuka Ishihara.* Santa Fe, NM: From Here Press, 1997.

Lebra, Joyce, Joy Paulson and Elizabeth Powers, eds. *Women in Changing Japan.* Boulder: Westview Press, 1976.

Lowitz, Leza, Miyuki Aoyama, Akemi Tomioka, eds. and trans. *A Long Rainy Season (Haiku & Tanka): Contemporary Japanese Women's Poetry,* vol. 1. Berkeley: Stone Bridge Press, 1994.

Mayhew, Lenore. *Monkey's Raincoat: Linked Poetry of the Bashō School with Haiku Selections.* Tokyo: Charles E. Tuttle Company, 1985.

Miner, Earl. *Japanese Linked Poetry: An Account with Translations of Renga and Haikai Sequences.* Princeton: Princeton University Press, 1979.*

Miner, Earl, and Hiroko Odagiri, trans. *The Monkey's Straw Raincoat and Other Poetry of the Bashō School.* Princeton: Princeton University Press, 1981.

Miner, Earl, Hiroko Odagiri, and Robert E. Morrell. *The Princeton Companion to Classical Japanese Literature.* Princeton: Princeton University Press, 1985.

Miyamori, Asataro. *An Anthology of Haiku, Ancient and Modern.* Tokyo: Maruzen, 1932.*

Nakane, Chie, and Shinzaburo Oishi, eds. *Tokugawa Japan: The Social and Economic Antecedents of Modern Japan.* Conrad Totman, trans. Tokyo: University of Tokyo Press, 1990.

Oseko, Toshihara. *Bashō's Haiku: Literal Translations for Those Who Wish to Read the Original Japanese Text, with Grammatical Analysis and Explanatory Notes.* Tokyo: Maruzen Co., Ltd., 1990.*

Porter, William N., tr. *A Year of Japanese Epigrams*. London: Oxford University Press, 1911.*

Rexroth, Kenneth, and Ikuko Atsumi. *The Burning Heart: Women Poets of Japan*. New York: Seabury Press, 1977.*

Rosenfield, John M. *The Courtly Tradition in Japanese Art and Literature*. Tokyo: Kodansha Publishers, 1973.*

Ross, Nancy Wilson. *The Way of Zen*. New York: Pantheon Books, 1957.

Sato, Hiroaki. *One Hundred Frogs: From Renga to Haiku to English*. New York: Weatherhill, 1983.*

Sato, Hiroaki, and Burton Watson. *From the Country of Eight Islands: An Anthology of Japanese Poetry*. New York: Columbia University Press, 1981.*

Sawa, Yuki, and Edith Schiffert, eds. and trans. *Haiku Master Buson*. Union City, CA: Heian International, 1978.

Stewart, Harold. *Net of Fireflies: Japanese Haiku and Painting*. Tokyo: Charles E. Tuttle Company, 1960.*

____*Chime of Windbells: A Year of Japanese Haiku*. Tokyo: Charles E. Tuttle Company, 1969.*

Stryk, Lucien. *On Love and Barley: Haiku of Bashō*. New York: Penguin Books, 1985.

Suzuki, Daisetz T. *Zen and Japanese Culture*. Princeton, NJ: Princeton University Press, 1959.*

Totman, Conrad. *Early Modern Japan*. Berkeley: University of California Press, 1993.

Trungpa, Chogyam. *Cutting Through Spiritual Materialism*. Berkeley: Shambhala Publications, 1973.

Ueda, Makoto. *Matsuo Bashō*. Tokyo: Kodansha International, 1970.

____*Bashō and His Interpreters: Selected Hokku with Commentary*. Stanford: Stanford University Press, 1992.

____*Literary and Art Theories in Japan*. Cleveland: Western Reserve University Press, 1967.

Waley, Arthur. *Japanese Poetry: The Uta*. Honolulu, HI: University of Hawaii Press, 1976.

Walsh, Clara A. *The Master Singers of Japan: Being Verse Translations from the Japanese Poets*. London: John Murray, 1910.*

Yamane, Tadashi. Yoshie Ishibashi and Patricia Donegan, trans. *Chiyo-jo's Haiku Seasons.* Kanazawa: Hokkoku Publishers, 1996.*

Yasuda, Kenneth. *The Japanese Haiku: Its Essential Nature, History and Possibilities in English, with Selected Examples.* Tokyo: Charles E. Tuttle Company, 1957.*

Yuasa, Nobuyuki. *Bashō's The Narrow Road to the Deep North and Other Travel Sketches.* Middlesex, England: Penguin Books, 1966.

Zolbrod, Leon M. *Haiku Painting.* Tokyo: Kodansha International, 1982.

IN JAPANESE

Chiyo-ni's Works:

Chiyo-ni Kushū 千代尼句集 (Collected Haiku of Chiyo-ni) Mugaian Kihaku, ed. 無外庵既白. Kyoto: Koto Tachibanaya Jihei, Toto Yamazaki Kinbei, 1764.

Haikai Matsu no Koe 俳諧松の声 (Haiku: Voice of the Pine) Mugaian Kihaku, ed. 無外庵既白. Kyoto: Koto Tachibanaya Jihei, 1771.

Himenoshiki 姫の式 (Princess Ceremony) Toro, ed. 兎路, 1726.

Chiyo-ni's Prefaces:

Bakusui 麦水, *Uzura-dachi* 鶉立, 1763.

Buson 蕪村, *Haikai Tamamoshū.* 俳諧玉藻集, 1774.

Chiseki 千尺, *Hishū Jukkei Emaki* 飛州十景絵巻, 1765.

Haikai Makarikane 俳諧まかりかね (*Saijiki*—seasonal reference book), 1771.

Kenpū 見風, *Kasumi Kata* 霞かた, 1763.

Kirai 几らい, *Yoriai Haiku Cho* 寄合俳句帖, 1774.

Secondary Sources:

Aida, Noritsugu 会田範次, Harada, Haruno 原田春乃, "Chiyo-jo" 千代女 in *Kinsei Joryū Bunjinden* 近世女流文人伝 (Stories of Women Writers in the Edo Period). Tokyo: Meiji Shoin, 1960.

Anonymous, "Hito-Watashi no Sokuseki—Nakamura Teijo" ひとわたしの足跡一中村汀女 in *Libre Magazine* りぶる (February, no. 47). Tokyo: Liberal Democratic Party, 1986.

Bessho, Makiko 別所真紀子、*Bashō ni Hirakareta Haikai no Joseishi Rokuju-rokunin no Komachi-tachi* 芭蕉にひらかれた俳諧の女性史 66 人の小町たち (Women's History of Haiku Opened by Bashō: Sixty-six Women). Tokyo: Origin Shuppan Center, 1989.

_____ 別所真紀子, *Kotoba o Te ni Shita Shisei no Onnatachi*「言葉」を手にした市井の女たち (Ordinary Women Who Acquired Words). Tokyo: Origin Shuppan Center, 1993.

Chōmu, ed. 蝶夢、*Seshu Meiroku Hokkushū* 施主名録発句集 (Daimyo Haiku Collection), 1770.

Fudeuchi, Yukiko 筆内幸子、*Kaga no Chiyo* 加賀の千代 (Chiyo of Kaga). Kanazawa: Hokkoku Shuppansha, 1984.

Hasegawa, Kanajo 長谷川かな女、*Kaga no Chiyo* 加賀の千代 (Chiyo of Kaga) rev. ed. Tokyo: Ikuei Shoin, 1986.

Hori, Nobuo 堀信夫, "Chiyojo" 千代女 (Chiyo-jo) in *Kenkyū Shiryō Nihon Koten Bungaku 7* 研究資料日本古典文学7 (Vol. 7: Study Materials of Classical Japanese Literature). Tokyo: Meiji Shoin, 1984.

Horikiri, Minoru 堀切実, *Bashō no Monjin* 芭蕉の門人 (Disciples of Bashō). Tokyo: Iwanami Shoten, 1991.

Ichikawa, Genzō ed., 市川源三, *Nihon Josei Bunka Shi* 日本女性文化史 (Japanese Women's Cultural History, vol. 2). Tokyo: Zenkoku Koto Gakko-Cho Kyokai, 1938–39.

Ishida, Motosue 石田元季, *Haibungaku Ronkō* 俳文学論考 (Essays on Haiku Literature). Tokyo: Yotokusha, 1944.

Kamitani, Hisayuki 紙谷久之, "Sōfū no Infu" 草風の印譜 (Sign of the Grass Breeze) in *Kyōdo to Bunka* 郷土と文化 vol. 11, 1984.

_____ 紙谷久之, "Chiyo-jo no Gayū Uchiyama Ippō" 千代女の雅友内山逸峰 (Chiyo-jo's Friend, Uchiyama Ippō) in *Kyōdo to Bunka* 郷土と文化 vol. 13, 1986.

_____ 紙谷久之, "Chiyo-ni no Iku Shōryōki" 千代尼の遺句渉猟記 (Finding Chiyo-ni's Haiku) in *Kyōdo to Bunka* 郷土と文化 vol. 15, 1989.

Katen, ed. 花顛, *Zoku Kinsei Kijinden* 続近世奇人伝 (Edo's Famous People, vol. 2), 1798.

Katō, Shūson 加藤秋邨, Ōtani, Atsuzō 大谷篤蔵, Imoto, Noichi 井本農一, *Haibungaku Daijiten* 俳文学大辞典 (Haiku Literature Dictionary). Tokyo: Kadokawa Shoten, 1995.

Katsumine, Shinpū 勝峯晋風, *Keishū Haika Zensbū* 閨秀俳家全集 (Complete Works of Women Haiku Poets). Tokyo: Shueikaku, 1922.

Kawashima, Tsuyu 川島つゆ, *Joryū Haijin* 女流俳人 (Women Haiku Poets). Tokyo: Meiji Shoin, 1957.

_____ 川島つゆ, "Chiyo-ni" 千代尼 in *Haiku Kōza* 8 俳句講座8 (vol. 8, Lectures on Haiku). Tokyo: Meiji Shoin 1959.

Kōkō, ed. 康工, *Haikai Hyakuichi-Shū* 俳諧百一集 (One Hundred and One Haiku Poets Collection), 1765.

Konishi, Jinichi 小西甚一, "Haiku no Sekai" 俳句の世界 (The World of Haiku) in *Kōdansha Gakujutsu Bunko* 1159 講談社学術文庫1159 (Kodansha Academic Library). Tokyo: Kodansha Ltd., 1995.

Kyoshi, Takahama 高濱虚子, *Haiku Dokubon* 俳句読本 (Haiku Book). Tokyo: Shinjusha, 1977.

Maruyama, Kazuhiko 丸山一彦, "Kaga no Chiyo" 加賀の千代 (Kaga no Chiyo) in *Nihon Joryū Bungakushi* 日本女流文学史 (History of Japanese Women's Literature). Tokyo: Dobun Shoin, 1970.

Matto City Central Library, ed. 松任市中央図書館, *Kaga no Chiyo Sankō Bunken-shū*, vol. 2 加賀の千代参考文献集、第二集 (List of Reference Books on Kaga no Chiyo, vol. 2), 1992.

Mizuhara, Shūōshi 水原秋桜子, Katō, Shūson 加藤秋邨, Yamamoto, Kenkichi 山本健吉, *Nihon Dai Saijiki* 日本大歳時記 (Japanese Seasonal Reference Dictionary). Tokyo: Kodansha, 1981.

Nakamoto, Jodō 中本恕堂, *Chiyo-ni no Isshō* 千代尼の一生 (The Life of Chiyo-ni). Matto: Hakusanginsha, 1932.

_____ 中本恕堂, *Chiyo-ni no Isshō* 千代尼の一生 (The Life of Chiyo-ni). Matto: Committee for Chiyo-ni's 150th year commemorative festival, 1935.

_____ 中本恕堂, *Kaga no Chiyo Kenkyū* 加賀の千代研究 (A Study of Chiyo of Kaga). Kanazawa: Hokkoku Shuppansha, 1970.

_____ 中本恕堂, *Kaga no Chiyo Zensbū* 加賀の千代全集 (Chiyo of Kaga's Complete Works) rev. ed. Kanazawa: Hokkoku Shuppansha, 1983.

_____ 中本恕堂, *Kaga no Chiyo Shinsekishū* 加賀の千代真蹟集 (A Collection of Chiyo of Kaga's Original Paintings), rev. ed. Kanazawa: Hokkoku Shuppansha, 1983.

Nakano, Tō-u 中野塔雨, *Kaga no Chiyo* 加賀の千代 (Chiyo of Kaga). Kanazawa: Hokkoku Shuppansha, 1974.

Nakano, Tatsuichi 中野辰一, "Chiyo-jo no Haiku Sōkō Zakkan" 千代女の「俳句草稿」雑感 (Various Impressions of Chiyo-ni's Own Notes on Her Own Haiku), in *Kyōdo to Bunka* 郷土と文化 vol. 10, 1983.

Satō, Kazuo 佐藤和夫, *Haiku kara Haiku e* 俳句からHAIKUへ (From Haiku to Haiku). Tokyo: Nanundo, 1987.

_____佐藤和夫, *Umi o Koeta Haiku* 海を超えた俳句 (Haiku Across the Sea), Maruzen Library 012. Tokyo: Maruzen, 1991.

Shida, Yoshihide 志田義秀, "Chiyo-ni o Meiseizuketa Ikku" 千代尼を名声づけた一句 (A Haiku Which Made Chiyo-ni Famous) in *Haibungaku no Kōsatsu* 俳文学の考察 (A Study of Haiku Literature). Tokyo: Meiji Shoin, 1932.

Shinagawa, Suzuko 品川鈴子, "Joryū Haikai—Shisen-jo to Chiyo no Kasen 'Hototogisu no Maki Kanshō'" 女流俳諧―紫仙女とちよの歌仙「ほととぎすの巻鑑賞」 (Women's Haiku—Shisen-jo and Chiyo's Kasen "Hototogisu") in *Renku Nenkan* 連句年鑑 (Renku Yearbook), 1988.

Shiromaru, Akira 城丸章, *Chiyo-ni* 千代尼 (Chiyo-ni). Matto: Shokoji Office, 1910.

Sōma, Gyofū 相馬御風, "Kaga no Chiyo" 加賀の千代 (Chiyo of Kaga) in *Teishin to Chiyo to Rengetsu* 貞心と千代と蓮月 (Teishin, Chiyo, and Rengetsu). Tokyo: Shunjusha, 1930.

Tonoda, Ryōsaku 殿田良作, "Kaga no Chiyo-jo no Kekkon ni tsuite" 加賀の千代女の結婚について (The Marriage of Kaga no Chiyo-jo) in *Renga to Haikai* 連歌と俳諧 (Renga and Haikai), vol. 3, 1936.

Ueno, Sachiko 上野さち子, *Joryū Haiku no Sekai* 女流俳句の世界 (The World of Women Haiku). Tokyo: Iwanami Shoten, 1989.

Yamaguchi, Seishi 山口誓子, *Haiku Tensaku Kyōshitsu* 俳句添削教室 (Haiku Correction Class). Tokyo: Tamagawa Daigaku Shuppanbu, 1986.

Yamamoto, Fujie 山本藤枝, "Kaga no Chiyo" 加賀の千代 in *Nihon no Joseishi* 日本の女性史 (History of Japanese Women, vol. 4). Tokyo: Shueisha, 1974.

Yamamoto, Kenkichi 山本健吉, *Junsui Haiku* 純粋俳句 (Pure Haiku). Tokyo: Sōgensha, 1952.

_____山本健吉, ed. *Haiku Kanshō Saijiki* 俳句鑑賞歳時記 (A Seasonal Reference Contemplation on Haiku). Kadokawa Shoten, 1993.

_____山本健吉, ed. *Kuka Saijiki* 句歌歳時記 (A Seasonal Reference), 4 vols. Shinchosha, 1986; paperback ed., 1993

Yamanaka, Rokuhiko 山中六彦, *Chiyo-jo to Kikusha-ni* 千代女と菊舎尼 (Chiyo-jo and Kikusha-ni). Tokyo: Jinbun Shoin, 1942.

Yamane, Tadashi 山根公, *Matto no Haijin Chiyo-jo* 松任の俳人千代女 (Matto's Poet Chiyo-jo). Matto: Matto City, 1993.

_____山根公, "Kaga no Chiyo no Hitogara to Kufū Hairon" 加賀の千代の人柄と句風俳論 (Chiyo of Kaga's Character and Her Haiku Style) in *Kyōdo to Bunka* 郷土と文化 vol. 4, 1977.

_____山根公, "Kaga no Chiyo ni Kan-suru Sho Mondai" 加賀の千代 に関する諸問題 (Various Problems of Kaga no Chiyo) in *Kyōdo to Bunka* 郷土と文化 vol. 6, 1979.

_____山根公, "Sakajiriya Karyō-ni to Chiyo-jo no Kōyū" 坂尻屋珈涼尼と千代女の交友 (Karyō-ni and Chiyo-ni's Relationship) in *Kyōdo to Bunka* 郷土と文化 vol. 12, 1985.

_____山根公, "Chiyo-ni to Matto no Haidan" 千代尼と松任俳壇 (Chiyo-ni and Matto's Haiku World) in *Kyōdo to Bunka* 郷土と文化 vol. 17, 1990.

Yoshimatsu, Yūichi 吉松祐一, *Kaga no Chiyo-jo no Shōgai* 加賀の千代女の生涯 (The Life of Chiyo-jo of Kaga). Tokyo: Daidokan Shoten, 1929.

"Books to Span the East and West"

Tuttle Publishing was founded in 1832 in the small New England town of Rutland, Vermont [USA]. Our core values remain as strong today as they were then—to publish best-in-class books which bring people together one page at a time. In 1948, we established a publishing outpost in Japan—and Tuttle is now a leader in publishing English-language books about the arts, languages and cultures of Asia. The world has become a much smaller place today and Asia's economic and cultural influence has grown. Yet the need for meaningful dialogue and information about this diverse region has never been greater. Over the past seven decades, Tuttle has published thousands of books on subjects ranging from martial arts and paper crafts to language learning and literature—and our talented authors, illustrators, designers and photographers have won many prestigious awards. We welcome you to explore the wealth of information available on Asia at **www.tuttlepublishing.com**.

Published by Tuttle Publishing, an imprint of Periplus Editions (HK) Ltd.

www.tuttlepublishing.com

Copyright © 2025 Patricia Donegan and Yoshie Ishibashi

Frontispiece: A detail from an ukiyoe woodblock print, *Chiyo-jo* (ca. 1843–1847) by Utagawa Kuniyoshi (1798–1861), from the series "Kenyū Fujo Kagami" (Reflections of Wise and Brave Women), Museum of Fine Arts, Springfield, Massachusetts, Raymond A. Bidwell Collection. Used by permission.

All rights reserved. No part of this publication may be reproduced or utilized in any form or by any means, electronic or mechanical, including photocopying, recording, or by any information storage and retrieval system, without prior written permission from the publisher.

Library of Congress Cataloging-in-Publication Data in process

ISBN 978-4-8053-1866-9

TUTTLE PUBLISHING® is a registered trademark of Tuttle Publishing, a division of Periplus Editions (HK) Ltd.

Distributed by

North America, Latin America & Europe
Tuttle Publishing
364 Innovation Drive, North Clarendon
VT 05759-9436 U.S.A.
Tel: 1 (802) 773-8930
Fax: 1 (802) 773-6993
info@tuttlepublishing.com
www.tuttlepublishing.com

Asia Pacific
Berkeley Books Pte. Ltd.
3 Kallang Sector, #04-01
Singapore 349278
Tel: (65) 67412178
Fax: (65) 67412179
inquiries@periplus.com.sg
www.tuttlepublishing.com

Japan
Tuttle Publishing
Yaekari Building, 3rd Floor
5-4-12 Osaki Shinagawa-ku
Tokyo 141 0032 Japan
Tel: 81 (3) 5437 0171
Fax: 81 (3) 5437 0755
sales@tuttle.co.jp
www.tuttle.co.jp

28 27 26 25   5 4 3 2 1   2503CM
Printed in China